PRAYING THROUGH AN *Adoption*

Wisdom, Encouragement, and Strategies for Your Journey

JACQUI JACKSON M.ED.

ANCHORING HOPE PUBLISHING

Praying Through an Adoption

This book contains material from the author's previous work, *God's Got This*, self-published in 2017.

Published by: Anchoring Hope Publishing
Cover by: Hello Delaney
Interior Design by: Step In Hope LLC
Interior images used under license from Shutterstock.com
NadyaEugene/Shutterstock.com
Great19/Shutterstock.com

ISBN: 979-8-9853483-4-7
eISBN: 979-8-9853483-5-4

Printed and bound in the United States of America.

SOME OF THE MATERIAL IN *PRAYING THROUGH AN ADOPTION* WAS ORIGINALLY PUBLISHED IN AN EARLIER WORK BY THE AUTHOR TITLED *GOD'S GOT THIS*. THE FOLLOWING ARE TESTIMONIALS ABOUT THAT BOOK AND THE AUTHOR'S CHILD WELFARE ORGANIZATION, IGNITE HOPE.

Praise for *God's Got This* and Ignite Hope

"The journey of becoming an adoptive family requires preparation. Every aspect of your life needs to be equipped to be obedient to God's call. From the very first step to every intermediate step, it's about God's will and not your own. *God's Got This* reminds us to stay bathed in the Word and in prayer. For where I am weak He is strong, and His strength will see us through."

Dr. Sharen Ford
Director for Foster Care and Adoption at Focus on the Family

"There are just no words to describe the impact that Ignite Hope has had on not only my agency, but for me personally. Working alongside Jacqui and getting to know her and her heart is a blessing of its own, but as I continue to learn about the work that Ignite Hope does and the passion that she has for serving others, it is truly humbling to say that I can call her my friend.

"Since meeting Jacqui, she has become one of our strongest allies for kids and families experiencing the foster care system. There is never an 'ask' too big or too small – they simply want to help and be a blessing to others. Mission accomplished! I've always heard that one drop of water can impact an entire ocean... to me, Jacqui is that one drop of water."

Brooke Ford, Cherokee County Director
Georgia Division of Family & Children Services

"As a mom to 28 children, 3 biological, 24 of which are adopted, and 1 that God simply knit our hearts together, I can vouch for the desperate need of support and prayer as you travel your parenting journey on any level. Jacqui's book will inspire, encourage, and ultimately challenge you to keep on persevering in your God ordained task of caring for His little ones, because truly *God's Got This*!"

Bonnie Walker, Author
Refuge Ranch: A Story For His Glory and
Refuge Ranch: The Glory Continues

"As you read this book, you will clearly see Jacqui's heart for adoption and for those who are called by God to walk this journey. Her perspective as both an adoptee and an adoptive mom is invaluable to anyone who is praying about or actively involved in the adoption process. The nuggets shared by her husband, Jeff, are also both insightful and encouraging. What I love most about this book is how it continues to point the reader to God's Word and how it focuses on the power and importance of prayer. As you follow God's leading to adopt, let this book challenge and equip you for the journey."

Chris Johnson
National Director of Church Partnerships
Lifeline Children's Services

"The work of Ignite Hope is indispensable for our family. We adopted a young girl almost six-years ago, but she passed away due to her medical special needs. Ignite Hope walked with us, prayed for us, and encouraged us through our grief journey. That work helped our family feel confident enough to emerge from tragedy and decide to follow God's call to adopt again. Ignite Hope's work continues in prayer, support, and inspiration as we travel that road again. This devotional guide will help you connect with Jacqui Jackson's passion for at-risk children and God's heart for adoption. I offer my highest recommendation."

Rev. Dr. Mark S. Jordan
Senior Pastor, Hope United Methodist Church, Dallas, Georgia

“As I read through her poignant and timely book, I felt like she was sitting next to me encouraging me through each step of the adoption of my son. The adoption process can be very lonely and isolating. It can feel as though very few understand the details involved and the grueling wait. Yet, as I read through the chapters Jacqui had written with her raw honesty, I began to feel seen and loved by my Creator. My approach to praying for my adoptive child changed course as a result of Jacqui's book.

“Your book was such a gift to me.”

Dr. Keith and Lavinia Meyers
Ignite Hope Board of Directors
Core Faculty at Walden University

DEDICATION

To my Momma & Daddy—Your lasting legacy of faith, family, and forever love just blesses me, the Hubs, and all our littles. I cannot imagine my life without y'all. I pray this effort makes you proud, knowing that your obedience so many years ago changed the trajectory of each of our lives. I love you both more than I can ever say. Momma—I can't wait to hug you again in Heaven. It's not goodbye—it's "see you soon!"

To my Littles—Each of you has taught me something I could learn from no one else—faithfulness, prayerfulness, the need to play, and the importance of prioritizing snuggle time together. Y'all made me a momma—the heart dream of my life. I love each of you recklessly. I pray daily, and even hourly, with great joy over the trajectory of your lives, your choices, and those you choose to love. Each of you has such an incredible calling and I can't wait to watch you walk into whatever God has prepared for you—big, wonderful plans. And they will be good! Always remember—Daddy and I love you to the moon and back and God loves you even more—no matter what!

To Chachi—my gift from God. You are my prayer warrior, my best friend, my lover, and my life. You see in me so much more than I see in myself. I cannot even imagine where I would be if God had not gifted me with you. You are infinitely more obedient, prayerful, and stronger than I will ever be, and I am so grateful for your leadership in our home and your submission to our Savior. I love you forever and always.

Love,
Jacqui

CONTENTS

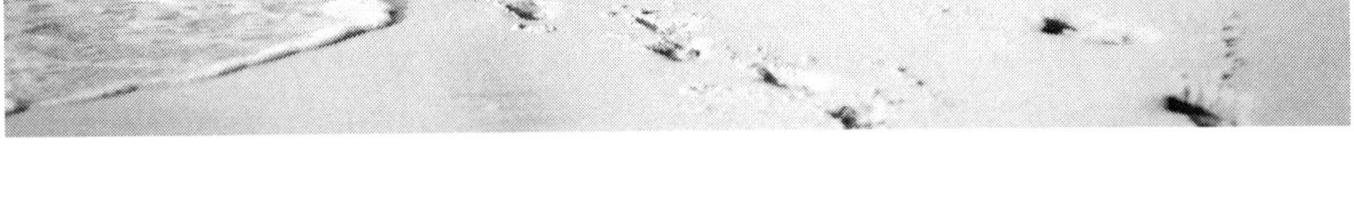

HOW TO USE THIS PRAYER GUIDE

The chapters in this book are presented in the order Holy Spirit downloaded them to me. However, please use this prayer guide in the way it will most benefit you. Start in the middle if a particular chapter title speaks to you. Take a peek at the end to learn about adoptive language. Or read it from start to finish if that is the best way for you to process it.

Above everything else, I encourage you to pray through what I've shared in these pages. Some information might not apply to you, but God may have you use it to encourage a parent walking this journey behind you.

If what you thought was coming does not pan out, go back to specific sections that speak to that wait or that hurt. It is okay to grieve. It is okay to celebrate. It is honestly okay to have all the emotions at once! God made us emotional but does not want us to be led around by our emotions.

When things feel too big or too hard, go back and reread the notes you wrote in your Action Points. Memorize the scripture that was shared. Reread or personalize the prayers we included. The TRUTH of God's Word will always speak louder than culture can shout. The Holy Spirit will speak words of comfort and joy in the hard and in the messy with His still, small voice.

I pray you will quiet your soul enough during this adoption roller coaster to hear your Father God speak to you personally and often.

Love,
Jacqui Jackson, M.Ed
CEO Ignite Hope

INTRODUCTION

Dear Reader and Friend,

Five years ago, with the gift of pregnancy insomnia, I wrote *God's Got This: A Strategic Prayer Guide for Your Adoption Journey.* As an adoptee, an adoptive sister, and an adoptive momma and biological momma—now twice over—I realized I had a unique perspective on adoption that needed to be shared. And since then, thousands have been encouraged and have received hope as they've read about and walked this journey behind me.

When we updated and expanded the book, we added several new chapters with content today's adopting families need to know. We changed the layout to make it easier to read and we added journal pages where you can record your own notes, thoughts, and prayers. We also included a section on the Language of Adoption. This content shares more sensitive and appropriate adoption terms to use that will better honor the child, the first family, and YOU!

There were so many changes and additions that we felt it was a totally different—and much better—book. So we decided it needed a new title. Welcome to *Praying Through an Adoption: Wisdom, Encouragement, and Strategies for Your Journey.*

I pray that sharing parts of our story with you will give you the encouragement to press on when things feel hard, to keep doing the next right thing when the waiting feels unending, and to celebrate God's goodness once your personal miracle of family comes to fruition through the gift of Adoption.

God Bless!

Jacqui Jackson, M. Ed.
CEO of Ignite Hope
Wife to Jeff and Mommy to many
Atlanta, Georgia
2022

Chapter 1

A WORD TO THE WISE

When I began my very first adoption journey—as in I was the infant being adopted—this entire space was very different.

I was adopted internationally, but waaaaaay before the Hague Adoption Convention was ratified in 1995. Back then adoptions were both easier and less protected. For me personally, this was great news. My Momma had me in her loving arms when I was just weeks old. Nowadays this scenario is almost unheard of in adoption circles.

Unfortunately, some adoptees do not have stories quite like mine. Their stories are uniquely theirs. Everyone's story has beauty and pain mixed together. For some people, their wounds are deep and their hearts still hurt. But please remember, as you become more entrenched in this space and with these people—adoptive parents, birth parents, adoptees, foster youth—every single one of them...every single one of us is fearfully and wonderfully made.

God is writing a great big story and each of us is critically important. The concept of adoption was originally God's and it's one way we can understand grace and salvation here on earth. Because He adopted us. This idea may be a new concept to you, but if you search through scripture, you will find adoption, fostering, and caring for the fatherless as constant themes across both Old and New Testaments.

In our first few pages together, I'd love to just encourage you. No matter what details are involved in your family's story, God is in those exact details. Nothing surprises Him, and there is nothing He cannot redeem. There's a reason beauty from ashes is a thing, because that's the business God is in.

Some adoptees may share stories of grace and joy and trust and love. Others may feel alone, misunderstood, or angry. Some adoptive families had an easy-breezy journey and can't wait to do it again. Some families have walked an uphill battle to get their children home, and now are climbing mountains trying to help these same kids heal.

Your story will be yours. Full of joy. Full of pain. Full of the hope that only comes from the author of the family—Jesus Christ.

So, as you listen to other people share their experiences, just pray for wisdom and discernment. Take off the rose-colored glasses and recognize that this venture won't be all unicorns and rainbows. But just as truly, accept that God is using everything—even the hard stuff—for His children's good and for His Glory.

I pray these stories, these memories, and these prayers offer you hope! Praying for you as you walk out your journey.

Daddy's Take:

As we began to walk out our adoption journey, we heard stories from a lot of different people and received a variety of opinions and comments. Some family members were stressed by the idea of waiting to be chosen and encouraged us to pursue medical procedures instead of adoption. Some friends were lukewarm as we shared our exciting news. Others celebrated alongside us and cheered us along every step of the way.

This is just one of those seasons when you need to deliberately, intentionally fix your eyes upon Him. The enemy will tell you all sorts of reasons why this will be hard, financially taxing, or even scary. Keep your eyes on God and step forward in confidence and in faith. He is with you wherever you go.

Scripture for Your Journey:

Psalm 139:14
I praise you because I am fearfully and wonderfully made; your works are wonderful, I know that full well.

Proverbs 3:5–6
Trust in the LORD with all your heart, and do not lean on your own understanding. In all your ways acknowledge him, and he will make straight your paths.

Isaiah 61:3
...to bestow on them a crown of beauty instead of ashes, the oil of joy instead of mourning, and a garment of praise instead of a spirit of despair.

Joshua 1:9
God is with you wherever you go.

Prayer for Your Journey:

Dear God,

As I walk through this journey of family and caring for Your children, I ask that You give me Your eyes to see and Your ears to hear. Help me use wisdom to figure out what I need to take as counsel from another family's story and what I need to release. Tender my heart, Lord, to each person in this space—birth families, social workers, adoptive families, and everyone else. We are all called here to minister to Your children in some way. Prepare my parenting heart for the exact child or children You have chosen for our family. Release me from anxiety and fear, recognizing that you already know what my road looks like, and You love us all. In Your Precious Name we pray. Amen.

Action Points:

1. As you begin to get your feet wet in this world of orphan care, be aware of the responses to your decision. God may be using you to tender the hearts of others toward His kids. Or the Holy Spirit may be warning you through a reaction that this person does not need to know the salient details or information.
2. Find a safe community to share the real *feels*. Note: This won't be on social media. I'd even advise being careful about what you post on adoption boards, etc. Remember, everything you type is a digital footprint that your child will find one day. Honor these kiddos and their first families and God. Look! Your first parenting effort! Good job!
3. Pray through the concerns. It may be that wise counsel is showing you an area you need to pray into. So, pray it up. It could also be that

another person's fear is coming out in their words to you. If you ask God for discernment, He will give it to you. Lean on Him for your understanding.

4. Pray! Pray! Pray! And then pray some more!

NOTES

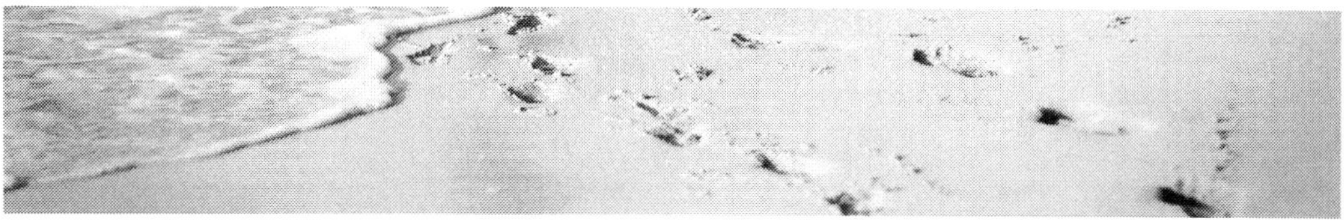

NOTES

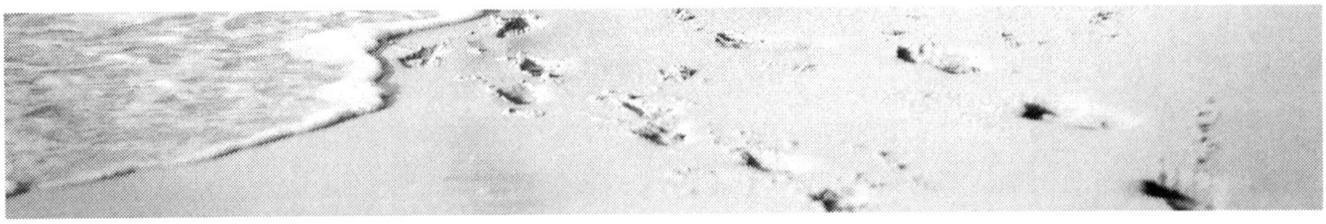

Chapter 2

CHOOSING YOUR PATH

Perhaps you have always known you were called to adoption. Maybe for you, like for me, toys like Cabbage Patch Dolls and Pound Puppies were more than a simple gift. Or perhaps you have come to this decision after years of wondering and wandering. However God has led you here, it is His clear leading. I want to encourage you with that first.

Sometimes Jesus speaks to us in parables, and other times He is just clear and simple. Well, my friends, this is one of those times. In James 1:27, God clearly states, "Religion that God our Father accepts as pure and faultless is this: to look after orphans and widows in their distress...." That, folks, is both a command and a commission. Add that to your total (okay, sometimes wavering) confidence. As crazy, difficult, or even surprising as others may find your calling, please remember that it is a heavenly, God-ordained invitation to join a joyous and, at times, overwhelming adventure.

So, strap in, pray hard, and get ready to go on the ride of your life. Welcome to your adoption journey.

Being an "adoptive mommy" is a title I wear gratefully, but one I use sparingly. You might think this was my natural "go to." But no, for me, it had to be supernatural. Facing an uphill infertility battle, I heard more than one doctor tell me that I had less than a 2% chance of conceiving and carrying. After leaving my teaching post at a Catholic school to pursue a last course of treatment, God let me hit my rock bottom. The nurse called and said the baby would not make it (again). Her advice to me was that the only next step was an expensive, invasive alternative, but I never felt called to walk that particular road. So where did that leave me? Weeping in a parking lot in Belmont, North Carolina. As I sobbed, I wondered how I could have reached this point. Then God intervened and drew near to me—His broken, bawling, hurting daughter—by using a sign. An *actual sign*, y'all! It was on the marquee of the old Baptist church in that small, southern town. It simply stated, "Moses was a basket-case, too." And I just froze.

Wait! Moses, the man called and chosen by God, was a hot mess just like me. Then God leveled me. Moses was also the first child to be adopted in the Bible.

During Biblical times, or, more specifically, Roman times, only adults were adopted (www.NewWorldEncyclopedia.org). Their reasoning was logical: Why adopt a child who may stray to the right or left? It made sense to adopt an adult who had proven his or her character and made wise life decisions. In this way, you'd know who he or she was; this was safer than waiting to find out who he or she would become. The idea of adoption as we know it now was rare at best. However, Moses, the author of Genesis, the man chosen to free God's people, began life as a persecuted minority and was transracially and transculturally adopted by none other than the princess of Egypt! God used this supernatural relationship unequivocally in Moses' life to accomplish His will for His Chosen People—the Israelites. Now tell me adoption isn't God-ordained!

I had hope in my heart and did a total 180-degree reverse in my perspective. It was as if I had been hit by lightning! Wow, Jacqui! I'd endured a full year of infertility testing, blood work, invasive procedures, and hormonal imbalances that could shame the sun. Now I realized that I could have prevented all of that if I had simply reflected on the life God had given me through the gift of adoption. On the other hand, though, God's timing is perfect. I wasn't ready to see it until I was ready to accept it. In God's infinite wisdom, He had allowed me free will. So, in yet another act of love, God waited until I was broken, until I was ready to accept His will in my life regarding my greatest heart's desire. And then He began to move in a mighty way.

Daddy's Take:

However you've come to consider an adoption journey, know you will never feel completely ready. You will never feel you have enough money or enough time. But, if God has called you to it, He will get you through it. So, take heart! God won't call you to adoption without calling your spouse, too. That is huge! Remain open, be prayerful, and listen to your wife's heart.

Scripture for Your Journey:

Hebrews 12:1–2
And let us run with perseverance the race marked out for us, fixing our eyes on Jesus, the pioneer and perfecter of faith. For the joy set before him he endured the cross, scorning its shame, and sat down at the right hand of the throne of God.

Exodus 2:10
When the child grew older, she took him to Pharaoh's daughter and he became her son. She named him Moses, saying, "I drew him out of the water."

Deuteronomy 1:30
The Lord your God, who is going before you, will fight for you....

Prayer for Your Journey:

Dear Heavenly Daddy,

You are the perfecter of our faith, but You are also the author of all life. You are writing an incredible story, and we praise You for allowing us to be part of it. Right now we are beginning a new part of that story as we consider and then begin to move confidently into an adoption journey. This will be a journey where we will need to rest in You, rely on You, and repeat almost daily, and possibly moment to moment over an unknown period of days, that You have ordained these steps. But You, Lord, have numbered our days. You have purposed every one of our steps under heaven.

Jesus, we boldly ask for You to come alongside us, to guide every one of these steps, and to lead us to our forever child. Open our hearts to Your call of adoption. Give us strength and confidence to follow Your command in James 1:27. We claim Your victory over this entire adventure. Amen.

Action Points:

1. Discuss the desire to adopt with your spouse. God will not call one and not the other.

2. Consider sharing your calling with other Godly counsel, such as parents, small group friends, and accountability partners. Wise counsel will help keep the wheels on this train, but foolish counsel will bring cultural naysayers into your calling. Be wise!
3. Consider praying and fasting separately and together about your next steps.

NOTES

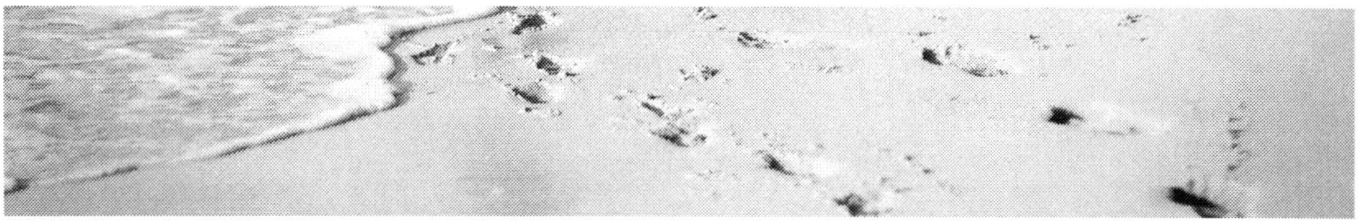

NOTES

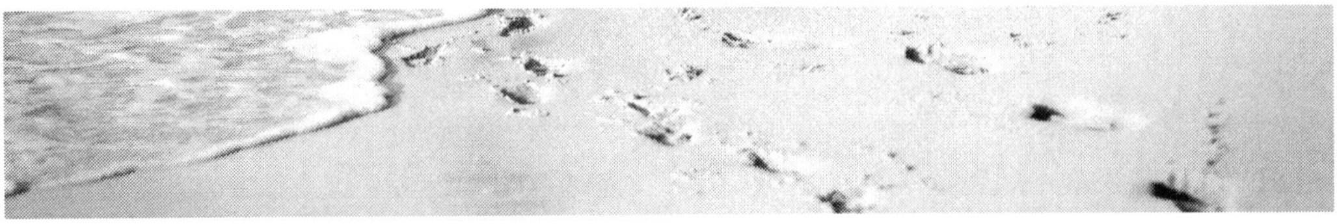

Chapter 3

WHO IS YOUR CHILD?

Well, the first step on your adoption journey is simply the decision to start. So, congratulations! If you are reading this section, then you are preparing your heart to move forward! Take a moment to bask in the miracle that will happen, and remember, "It is not if; it's when!" Cling to that. I found as I prayed through our family's adoptions that this next step was crucial, but it was hard! You have to be completely honest with yourself, your spouse, and, eventually, your agency or social worker. You have to get yourself in a position to be vulnerable and ready to listen to God's leading.

What, you may ask, is this huge next step? Quite simply, it is identifying who is supposed to be your child. While loving and creating a family through adoption is similar to a biological addition in many ways, there are key differences, and this is one. With a biological birth, to quote our daughter's preschool teacher, "You get what you get, and you don't pitch a fit." However, with an adoption, you get information, forms, and choices—and, if you are a bleeding heart like me, you will be ready and completely willing to take on a sickly, green flamingo if you can dress it up and teach it to say, "Mama!" But really, can you handle that bird?

When first faced with this question, I was sitting in a small agency's backroom preparing to saw off my right arm to find my child. I had a very wise and discerning social worker say something offensive, horrible, but yet so very true. "Jacqui," she said, "you must be brutally honest about who should be your child. You must consider what God has called you to handle." Then came the form.

It listed pretty much everything you can think of, ranging from addictions and mental illnesses to genetic diseases and specific tendencies. The special needs delineated made my head spin. I was so overwhelmed. I wanted a beautiful baby, so why in the world was I looking at every nightmare I had ever heard of written down on paper? That was when God leveled me. These children that were the heart and the face of each of these harsh realities were His children. My child-to-be was His child. He loved these children like He loves you and me. And He wanted the very best for them...and that best could be *me*!

Immediately my "But Lord," struck up! "But Lord, I can't handle this," and "But Lord, I am afraid," were immediate responses. And then, the most shameful thought: "But Lord, it's not what I pictured." That was a moment of realization. I was right where God wanted me to be. Admitting my dreams, and surrendering those for His better dreams, was a spiritual rite of passage I needed to experience.

With biological children, you don't have information. You don't know if your perfect little bundle will suffer a life-changing illness or an extreme accident. If everything goes splendidly for you genetically, you still don't know the free-will choices that child will make later. You simply don't know.

However, with adoption, you have some thoughts, ideas, and even labels, if you will. If I had a label for myself for my child to consider, it might look something like this: slightly neurotic, very emotional, child-obsessed, and sad. At that moment, all of those descriptions were accurate. My own life label didn't sing of overcoming, surrendering, or bringing God glory. It was simply the cry of my heart to find my family, just like those waiting children.

So be bold, be prayerful, and be honest. It is important to consider what you, your spouse, and your family can handle financially, medically, emotionally, and in terms of background. These are some difficult things to process, but you must contemplate them to be fair not only to yourselves, but more importantly, to your child.

This is not the time to be reserved. You are searching for your particular child. Wherever you are and however you feel right now, know that God gives graciously and generously. He may move you from your place of comfort, but He will give you everything you need to handle that.

Lastly, remember we don't adopt to rescue, we adopt because each of us was rescued the moment Christ died on the cross. It's His love in us that works out His love in the world through us. Adoption is one of God's divine examples of how He sacrificially loves each one of us! After all, He is our Adoptive Daddy.

As an important side note, make sure that the agency, adoption worker, or consultant you are working with gives you all the information you request, especially if you are waiting for an older child, sibling group, or an international placement. You may be experiencing information overload (there will be more on that later), but look out for certain red flags in the process. These red flags include any agency that is withholding information, giving skeletal background information, or not giving full disclosure regarding the birth family's level of commitment to an adoption placement.

Pray hard, for God promises wisdom if we ask for it. James 1:5–6 states, "If any of you lacks wisdom, you should ask God, who gives generously to all without finding fault, and it will be given to you. But when you ask, you must believe and not doubt, because the one who doubts is like a wave of the sea, blown and tossed by the wind." I am begging for wisdom and discernment for each of you, and He will hear this prayer.

Daddy's Take:

It's different for men than it is for women. Whereas I wanted to adopt, and I was hopeful for the adoption, my wife was on a mission. She knew that someone specific was missing from our family. She actually described our family at that moment as a puzzle with a missing piece. How could she not desperately love, want, and search for the missing one who would make our family complete? Outwardly, we processed differently; however, when I searched my heart, I realized what she said made sense. Her love for the child we didn't even know yet made me love her even more.

Scripture for Your Journey:

Psalm 25:4–5
Show me your ways, Lord,
teach me your paths.
5*Guide me in your truth and teach me,*
for you are God my Savior,
and my hope is in you all day long.

Psalm 31:3
Since you are my rock and my fortress,
for the sake of your name lead and guide me.

Prayer for Your Journey:

Dear Jesus,
This is a time when we need Your clear leading and guidance in ways we have never required before. We need to know whom You have chosen for our family, and we pray that our hearts are open to exactly that little soul. Our whole lives have prepared us in different ways to be parents to this specific child. We know our comfort levels, but we also know that through Your grace and mercy, You will give us the resources and strength to handle exactly whom You have chosen as best. So, Lord, that is what we humbly ask right now. Direct us to Your best, most perfect gift in the form of the child we love and are praying for You to lead to our home. Let us be honest with one another, and let us extend grace. We ask for discernment as we determine this, and we trust You with how this family will be pieced together. Thank You for loving us. But more than that, thank You for loving this child we haven't even met, knowing that You created this child as ours.
Amen.

Action Points:

1. What is your comfort level with interracial or intercultural adoption? What about international or domestic adoption?
2. What is your comfort level with a difficult birth family, medical difficulties, or other stretching situations?
3. How will your extended family receive this decision? (God works in extended families, just as He works in our own lives. Trust His leading. If some family members don't "get it," then that is not a reason to say no to this process. It is an opportunity for God to spiritually grow your extended family like He's chosen to physically grow your immediate family!)
4. Are there any circumstances or situations that truly scare you or that you feel unable to handle?
5. In light of your current family circumstances and financial responsibilities, what do you think you can handle? What can God enable you to handle?
6. Who is your dream child? (This is a moment of truth, and that's okay. Jesus knows that you may have always wanted a child with your sister's

button nose, a roly-poly infant, or a dainty bundle. Own that dream, but then release it. God's got this dream, and His gifts are good. Don't get held up by what you pictured; embrace God's picture! It is even better!)

NOTES

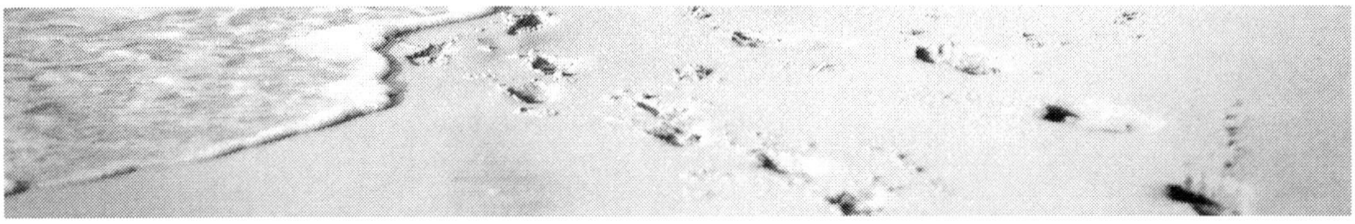

NOTES

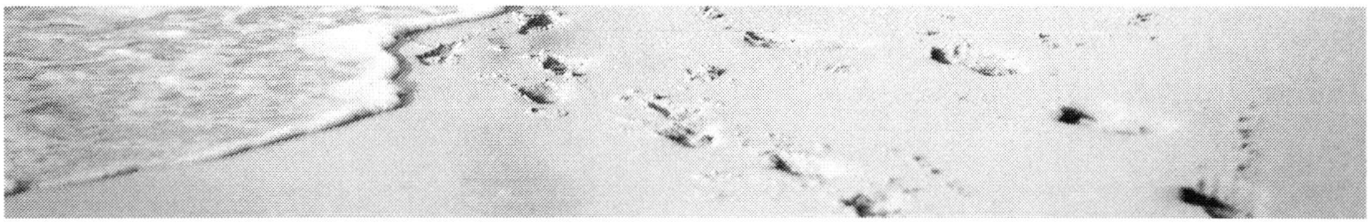

Chapter 4

WHERE IS YOUR CHILD?

I want to provide full disclosure from my personal experience: It seems to me that subsequent adoptions are more difficult than the first. The moment I decided to adopt the first time, I started telling everyone, and I mean everyone. No one was safe—the deli attendant at Publix, the cashier at Panera—everyone heard my plan! I was an absolutely glowing mother-to-be, even though I had no paperwork, no approval, no agency, and no "due date." But friend, I had a plan, and that plan gave me a sense of purpose.

I ran full tilt into that adoption and never looked back! The second adoption? Well, it was an uphill battle from the start. While I had been perfect on paper during the first adoption, life had intervened, and I had to put certain information on the forms that was less than ideal. God had me in His mighty hand the entire way, but I really got focused on my flesh, afraid I would be judged and found wanting in the parenting arena.

The path to our second child was nothing like the path to the first adoption! Nothing at all. And frankly, I was not so cool with that. I sat up late at night talking to God in a broken psalmist kind of way, not in a surrendered, peaceful manner. That's okay, though. A huge part of this journey was about deepening my relationship with God, which meant my faith was stretched, and I reacted accordingly. God was not surprised by my outbursts and fear. He was growing me, and He expected me to have growing pains. For me, it had to happen this way, or we would have never found our son.

So, where is your child?

Now that you have gotten a handle on who your child is, it is time to find out where your child is. For some of you, this is the easy part, for you have previous experience with a well-known, well-respected agency that worked for you in the past. It feels like a no-brainer to go there, right? I'd encourage you to pause and pray.

Although returning to something familiar is comfortable and may be exactly what you need to do, I would encourage you to get down on your knees and seek God's will in this. Adoptees and their families can face spiritual oppression, so it is important to be vigilant in prayer.

We have counseled so many heartsick families who were confused about where to go and how to proceed. Questions have included the following: Which country? Which agency? Which state? Open or closed or semi-open adoptions? What do any of these terms even mean?

First, let me encourage you: God's got this. Do not worry about all of the technical terminology and all of the steps that you must take to get your child home. Proverbs 3:5–6 says,

> 5 Trust in the Lord with all your heart
> and lean not on your own understanding;
> 6 in all your ways submit to him,
> and he will make your paths straight.

It is okay that you don't understand everything. God does. Rely on Him.

When my parents adopted me, they used a well-known agency for international adoptions. The time frame was like clockwork. They were matched with me and received their travel dates. Things were clicking along until they hit a wall of obstacles at the very end that made my adoption seem impossible—wait for it, it's a really good story! Even with the crazy at the end, they waded back into adoption waters two years later to begin the process again. They figured they had faced everything and were old hats at this baby game—but BOOM! Everything had changed. Here's a bit of my sister's story:

The fabulous agency they had previously used was no longer operating. My parents knew they wanted to return to Colombia, but they had no idea how to proceed without the safety net and professional counsel of their tried and true support system. So, they paused and prayed, and God led them forward into California's very first international identified placement; needless to say, this was rather scary. There they were, two hopeful parents-to-be, tilling previously untilled soil in the late 70's before adoption resources were widespread.

By the grace of God, they had remained very close to my foster mother, Marta, and they were also able to work with her later to adopt my sweet sister and best friend, Jessica. Marta represented my parents in-country, and she was even given Jessica's visas and paperwork. This allowed her to fly internationally into LAX bringing Jessica with her. It is unlikely that this could ever happen by today's standards.

If you have prayed and feel called to adoption, your job is to jump through the right hoops, crawl through the bureaucracy, and slice through the red tape, for each piece of paper in triplicate gets you that much closer to your newest addition. If you are hitting molehills that turn into mountains, that doesn't mean you're out of God's will; it means you are probably on the right path. If your heart is beaten down by obstacles and you are wondering why it's not easy, acknowledge that it could be spiritual opposition. Then pray the enemy away and keep on keepin' on. Whether you are facing spiritual opposition or not, Jesus has proven His victory over Satan and a broken world, so don't focus on the obstacles; just pray hard and keep on marching!

As a random aside, I once had an acquaintance say to me, "Oh you adopted? You had kids the easy way. No labor for you!" To that I say, "Bless her heart!" Having now walked down the road of biological progeny and adoption journeys, I will tell you two truths. First, adoption is a spiritual labor that has no set due date. With a biological child, you show up to your first appointment and they give you a due date and you are pretty sure plus or minus four weeks, you will be rewarded with a wrinkly, tiny person to love and nurture. With adoption, it can happen extremely quickly and relatively easily, or it can take what feels like an eternity. I have known friends that began and finished the entire process within six weeks; I have also known friends who were in the process for more than four years. The unknown is scary; just remember that the unknown to you is known to God.

With a physical labor you have the option of an epidural or other medically approved pain reliever; with an adoption, no such meds exist. It requires total reliance on the Father, on His perfect timing, and on your support system to literally prop you up when it feels like the weight of the world is about to crush you under the bulk of paperwork, interviews, and health approvals. So yes, nine months of physical changes can be so hard, for there is medical bed rest and there are endless days of nausea, but adoption is not for the faint of heart. As you begin to reflect on and process all the many ways that God's fingerprints are so clearly evident in every one of your preordained steps, you realize you are part of a miracle, and every ounce of glory goes to Him.

So pray, families. Your child awaits you. Just ask your Heavenly Daddy where to find him or her, and He will show you the way.

Daddy's Take:

My wife is one of the most prayerful people I have ever known. I try to keep up! Because of her obedience to Jesus, I believe that we have received some truly amazing answers and miracles right on time. Notice that I said right on time, not early! Don't give up just before the miracle!

Pray that God will direct you toward your child, the one whom God created especially for your forever family. If you have that God-given calling to adopt, but He hasn't put a location on your heart, it may just mean that it's time to take a step. Think of the story of the parting of the Jordan River: God did not part the waters until they took their first steps into the water.

Don't wait until you are sure you have the right answer. God may just be saying, "Take a step and I will guide your path!" Get ready to take that step! There are few regrets for those who have taken steps toward their adoption journey; there are many more regrets for people who look back and wish they had acted sooner.

Scripture for Your Journey:

Joshua 3:15–16
Now the Jordan is at flood stage all during harvest. Yet as soon as the priests who carried the ark reached the Jordan and their feet touched the water's edge, the water from upstream stopped flowing. It piled up in a heap a great distance away, at a town called Adam in the vicinity of Zarethan, while the water flowing down to the Sea of the Arabah (that is, the Dead Sea) was completely cut off. So the people crossed over opposite Jericho.

Psalm 32:8
I will instruct you and teach you in the way you should go;
I will counsel you with my loving eye on you.

Prayer for Your Journey:

Dear Jesus,
You direct our steps in the little and in the large, and this is one of the largest undertakings of our lives. Although it feels like a quest as we search out treasure amidst unknown obstacles and hindrances, You know exactly where our child is right now. As we pray over him or her, we ask You to place Your hedges of protection around our child, giving provision and peace, while we fight to find this little soul whom You have placed on our hearts. Lead us quickly, make us humble, and meet every need for our precious child as we begin this journey of hope. Amen and Amen.

Action Points:

1. Do you feel a connection or pull to a certain country, people, group, or specific area? Why?
2. After sharing your hopes with Godly counsel, are you feeling led in a particular direction, such as domestic or international?
3. Are you becoming strongly convinced of a location? Or conversely, do you believe that certain doors are closing? (That is okay—your child can't be everywhere at once. When a door closes, feel total peace that you are a step closer to finding your child, for it is narrowing your prayer area!)

NOTES

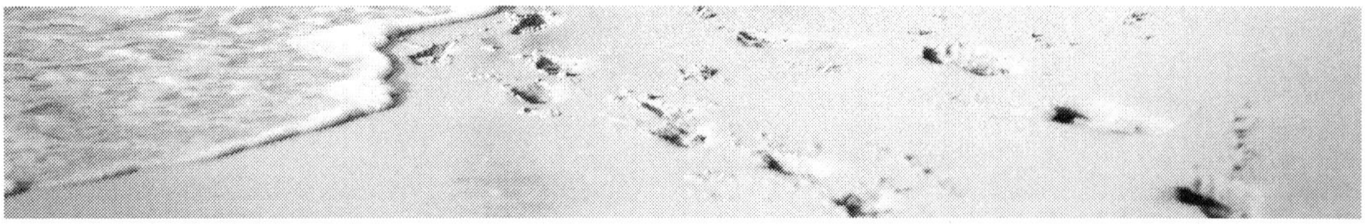

NOTES

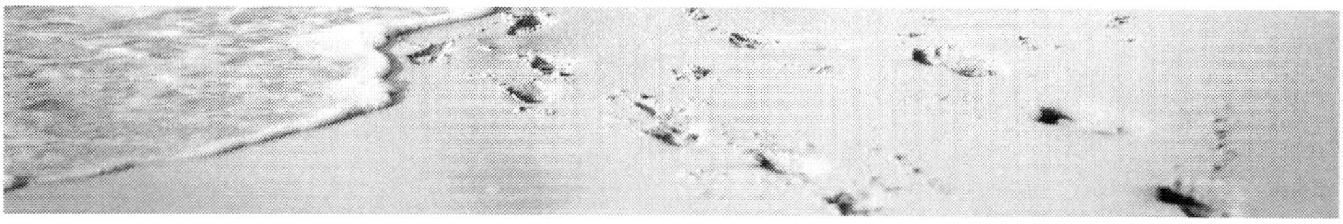

Chapter 5

IS YOUR CHILD IN FOSTER CARE?

Adoption is always a God-thing. Adopting a "Waiting Child" is a set-apart category in a space that is already replete with highs and lows. Currently, in America, there are over 430,000 kids in foster care, and about 120,000 of them are immediately available for an adoptive placement (AdoptUSKids.org, 2020). Lifeline Children's Services, a Christian adoption agency, says that waiting children "are older, have more significant medical special needs, or are a sibling group—all characteristics that often present difficulties in finding families" (LifelineChild.org, 2021).

Statistics compiled on childwelfare.gov reveal interesting trends in the foster care system. Between 2008 and 2018, adoptions out of foster care increased from 19% to 25%. This trend correlates with a decrease in international adoptions. By 2015, international adoptions had dropped 72 percent, to 12,000 in total. Just 5,500 of these children ended up in the U.S. (Mark Montgomery and Irene Powell, TheConversation.com, 2018).

Some of the shift internationally is due to widening views on adoption in many countries. For example, Chinese nationals began adopting and fostering their own children. This is truly a blessing. This shift is one of the reasons that the wait time for a placement from China has increased.

The shift domestically towards a higher rate of adoption has been equally surprising as of late. Although the goal of foster care is always reunification, there are times when this is not a tenable option. Studies have estimated that one in five children reenter foster care within five years of reunification (Brook & McDonald, 2009; Wulczyn, 2004). So, sometimes the courts may determine that adoption rather than reunification is in the child's best interest. At that point, they begin the process of TPR—or termination of parental rights.

I share these statistics prayerfully. First of all, these are children—not statistics. Every ONE of these kiddos is precious to Father God, and one (or more!) of these children may be YOURS! If you are well entrenched in the world of Orphaned and Vulnerable Children (OVC), none of this surprises you. However, if this is your first foray into this space, understanding that each of these numbers represents a little soul and a heart needing to be mothered and fathered, I say this to encourage you—these kids have been through a lot.

A child does not arrive at the place of adoption unless a lot of safeguards and protections have broken down. That, my friends, is a direct spiritual attack from the enemy. Not every kid faces this type of battle. Within Ignite Hope, we believe there is a reason why some children are attacked from the womb and that is because there is a kingdom calling upon their lives. The spiritual battle won't stop just because they enter your home. If anything, it could ramp up. But, take heart. Our God is more than equal to this challenge. And you, sweet friend, can do "all things through Christ who strengthens you" (Philippians 4:13).

There is an incredible testimony that comes from welcoming a waiting child into the home. I've had the privilege of walking beside several of our Ignite Hope families that had this calling on their lives. As I've shared previously, there are always pangs and twinges when adding a whole human being to an established family unit. It doesn't matter if that family unit consists of yourself, your fur baby, and your support system, or if your family make-up is a blended and blessed hodge-podge of ages and characteristics. It will take work. It will take heart work. But it will be so worth it.

If you decide that adopting a child currently in foster care is what God wants for your family, I challenge you to form a holistic picture of what your child has experienced. This will take asking many questions so you can learn your child's full social and medical history. I encourage you to find out about their home, community, culture, and anything else the Holy Spirit reveals is important to their grieving heart. The joy of having your child come home is precious, but there has been a loss. You all will need time to attach, to grow trust, and to establish a new normal.

I encourage you to ask for revelation—my favorite type of mothering prayer. Ask Jesus to reveal whatever it is you need to parent this child well, to understand and honor his or her first family, and to help your child heal. I have prayed this type of prayer numerous times during my years of motherhood, and God has always, always answered! Disclaimer: make sure you've checked your own heart because you may find out some hard things you weren't expecting. But, that is okay. None of this is a surprise to Jesus.

The adoption process requires help from all parts of the Trinity. As you dig deeper into scripture and your own faith, which by the way is an amazing byproduct of this journey, you will find that there are times when you need the comfort of Father God, the friendship of Jesus, or the leading of the Holy Spirit. Just know that although we serve a triune God, every single aspect of His heart is cheering you on as you learn how to parent in this space. And parent you will. There will be triumphs and there will be trials, but just know you are not doing this alone. The ultimate parent is walking right alongside you, and thank God for that!

Daddy's Take:

A few years ago, I spoke at a local church in May for National Foster Care Awareness month. As I shared from my heart what I've seen God do through our ministry, I emphasized that "Everyone Can Do Something." No matter where you are in your life journey, you can help at-risk kids. You may be the perfect "grandparents" for a newly placed child. You may be the cool "Aunt or Uncle" that can bless a growing family with babysitting, a night out, or a nap. I also encouraged fostering and adopting families to consider your family, your child(ren), and what you may need, recognizing your needs will shift, and that's okay. The best thing is to pray together and for you to be candid about the help you need.

Scripture for Your Journey:

Philippians 4:13, NKJV
I can do all things through Christ who strengthens me.

Psalm 68:6, NIV
God sets the lonely in families.

Prayer for Your Journey:

Dear Heavenly Father,
We ask that You grant us revelation as we learn to parent kids from hard

places. We ask for divine inspiration to know what will minister to their hearts and what might hurt. Help us to recognize and embrace that the ways we were parented may not work for our child, and that is okay. You are a creative creator. You are the author of the family. You have called this child by name. Help us as parents to become what this child needs, and, most importantly, help us to guide their hurting hearts to Your good Father's heart. Let them realize their worth as Your child. And thank You that now we can call this child ours. Amen.

Action Points:

1. Help your people understand the nuances in adopting a child who has been waiting for a family. You can share statistics, inspirational stories of God-Wins, and even the hard stuff. Be real but let God lead you in what and how much to share, specifically once you have been matched. It's much easier to have these conversations before you have the child in your home.
2. Be realistic with yourself. Release the unicorns and rainbows ideal and be ready to embrace the little joys. It may not be an immediate Brady Bunch-type situation with everyone singing in harmony, but celebrate their homecoming, the first meal, getting to put them to bed for the first time.
3. Have some backup ready when you need to take a break. Ask your people to consider gifting you with respite care, for an hour or an evening, whatever it may look like. You need to take care of yourself while you are caregiving.

NOTES

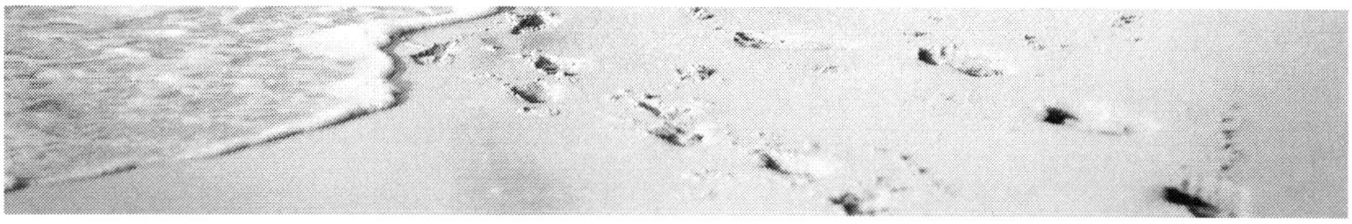

NOTES

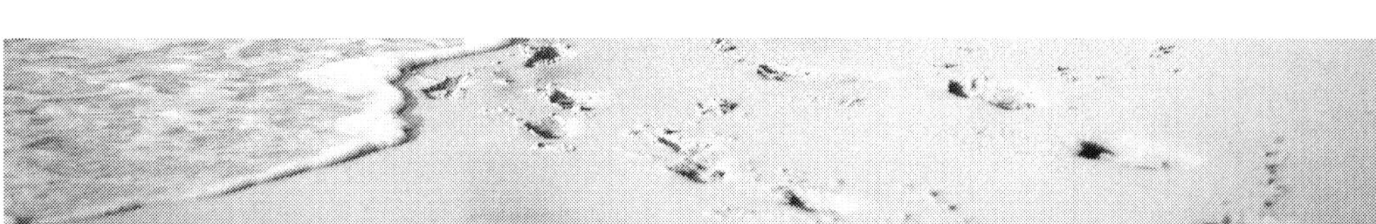

Chapter 6

PAPER PREGNANT

So, you've decided to adopt, searched your heart to determine "who" your child will be, and narrowed down the geographic location of your child. It's time to figure out the resources you will need to make this dream a reality. In other words, you need to find an agency, an adoption consultant, an attorney, or possibly all three in order to move forward.

One thing I would encourage you to do is to talk with other adoptive parents. There are blogs and support sites online, but I have found that reaching out to your community is even better for this leg of your journey. Let people know your plans, and watch how God uses His church to minister right to you. Personally, after deciding to adopt, I entered a state of confusion. I didn't really know what to do after telling everyone I was going to adopt. My dear daddy worked for a Christian think tank at the time. Daddy's boss and wife had adopted five times through the same Christian agency. Bingo! This agency worked, and apparently worked well, or why would they keep returning?

Then came the first obstacle. Very often agencies, especially those focused on domestic adoptions, have state-dependent expectations. For example, some states require that you live in the state where they are based. Fortunately, this agency had an office in South Carolina where the old homestead was situated, so that worked out nicely. (Thanks, God!)

I have had other friends who knew that they were specifically interested in an international placement and were directed by friends or family who previously walked a similar journey. Most recently, dear friends and cousins have used an adoption consultant that matched families with agencies or adoption attorneys nationally. There are so many ways to proceed that it feels totally overwhelming. Some states require medical paperwork, interviews, home visits, and fingerprinting before you can even be considered. Yes, I know, I know! It can feel impossible.

After years of prayer, and now a mommy to many, I've learned a few things. While a biological labor may last many hours or possibly days, the spiritual labor of adoption hits Mom and Dad (and possibly other family members) hard and without a definitive end in sight. With no due date, you may feel that you took a wrong turn somewhere. Please let me encourage you that the more uphill battles you face, the more likely you are on the right path.

Consider these truths: You have felt a calling from God. You have prayed extensively. You have consulted and listened to Godly counsel. You are actively walking out the will of God in His mandate found in James 1:27. So stand firm! You are expecting, and you are expecting something good!

By the time my husband and I finished the paperwork for our son (our first son and second adoption overall), I had a four-inch-thick stack of papers documenting my family's life. It was close to 50 pages of interview questions. It even included paperwork on our dog, for the vet had to sign off that Foxy Dawg, our three-pound canine wonder, could handle a new addition! As I was standing in the post office to mail the documents, God gave me a little hug. A godly friend walked into the post office who knew all the stress we had endured. Without any hesitation, her hands became Jesus' hands as she grabbed me and prayed over that important package. Listening to someone pray our child home gave me a peace I cannot explain.

As a little humor can't go awry when you are reading about daunting paperwork and possibly sitting over a stack of your own adoption documents, let me share this with you: In 1976, after a year of prayer and paperwork, my parents were matched with what they could only describe as the most amazing, wise, wonderful, and enchanting child in the world: yours truly. Although the photo the orphanage sent showed pillow prints on my face and only one eye opened, they knew beauty when they saw it. Momma especially was ready to run straight to South America to start hugging on me. But alas, someone somewhere misplaced my parents' FBI fingerprints.

Momma, in her sweet southern charm, called straight to the White House to get someone with clout and knowledge to help. Her baby was waiting, and fingerprints or not, she was heading south...and soon! After being passed from lowly aide to lowly aide, she said the magic words: "If I robbed a bank right now, I bet you'd have my fingerprints in no time. Now help me get my daughter!" I have no idea if the threat was received with grace and humor, if Momma simply found a kindred spirit, or if she was pushed up the chain because they did fear for the nation's banks, but she finally found someone who could expedite things. My parents traveled just days after the incident, and we all lived happily ever after. (And incidentally, this a blanket disclaimer—calling the White House to voice a threat in this day and age is probably not a great way to expedite your adoption process...just saying.)

My mother reminded me of that story when, 34 years later, our FBI fingerprints went missing. I went directly to the FBI. In an act of faith and possibly of desperation, my husband and I made a decision. We hopped on a plane to the Midwest without this necessary piece of information because I had been promised that our fingerprints had been sent. Thankfully, God once again moved adoption mountains and the adoption agency received the fingerprints. This just goes to show that God is in control!

Daddy's Take:

Adoption will prompt you to lean on God like never before! I had never felt so needy for God's grace as those moments when I had no idea what was going to happen next. God will come through. Just prepare for the unknown and be thankful no matter what.

When we flew west for our son, it was one of the most challenging times in our lives. We arrived in his town with three crippling burdens. First, the fingerprints weren't done yet (although God handled that quickly). Second, upon landing we received the news that while we were in the air, our son's circumstances had changed and he might not be available for adoption. Third, this shift in circumstances would now extend our travel time from five days to three weeks. With no extra money and no extra vacation from work, we were terrified.

We now had a choice. We could either pack it up and go home or drop to our knees and have faith that God's plan would work out! I am glad we picked the second choice.

Scripture for Your Journey:

Jeremiah 1:5
Before I formed you in the womb I knew you...

Psalm 100:3
Know that the Lord is God.
It is he who made us, and we are his;
we are his people, the sheep of his pasture.

Prayer for Your Journey:

Dear Father,
You are our father, and You are our child's father, too. Although we may not know this specific child yet, You do. Give us courage to walk by faith, both prayerfully and expectantly, as You work out the plan You have for each of us. Thank You for loving us as a Heavenly Daddy. Thank You for forming this child. Amen.

Action Points:

1. How does it feel to be going through spiritual labor pains of bureaucracy, paperwork, and waiting?
2. Do you feel connected to your spouse in this process? Just like with a biological birth, pretty much any and all feelings are normal!

NOTES

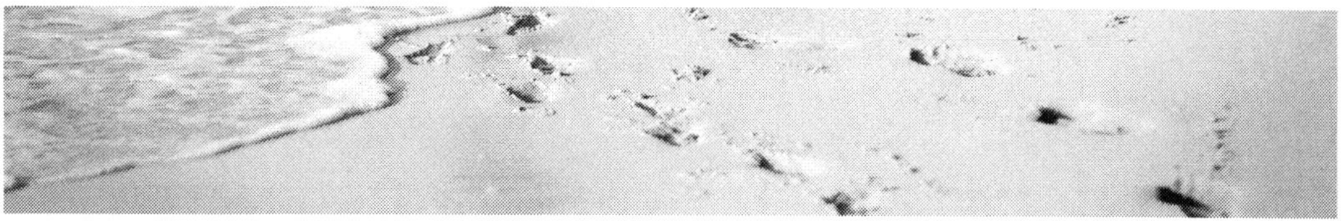

NOTES

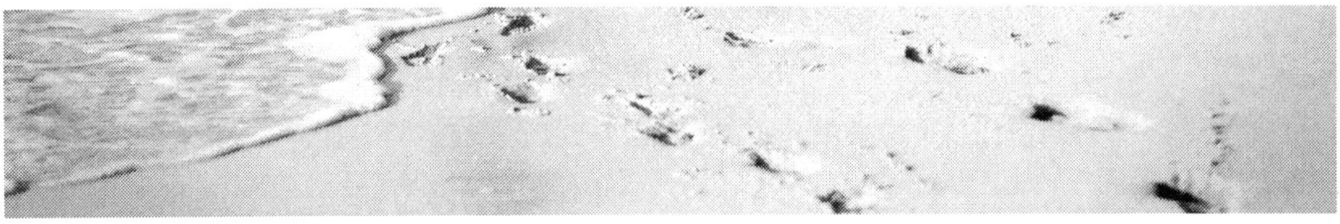

Chapter 7

WHEN YOU FEEL ALONE

My hope and prayer is that when you confirm in your heart that you are called to adoption, you hear heaven singing over you. I pray that your prayerful, present support system makes itself known in great joy. I hope that you find yourself the grateful recipient of kind words, encouragement, and offers to assist. For some of you, you will enjoy that blessing and it will seal the affirmation that this is your path.

Others may walk a slightly different path. Your family may not quite understand why you are "doing this." Friends who are not privy to your closest thought processes may be blatantly confused. Some people may choose to share with you the latest Lifetime-movie-of-the-week-type drama surrounding agencies or placements or wait times. If you meet up with these types of people or prognostications, I want to encourage you. God is NOT simply testing your obedience, and He is not telling you "No." More often than not, the obstacles we face in the natural world are the stepping stones for the steps God is preparing for us supernaturally. Do you want confirmation? Just look into His Word.

When I decided to adopt, I experienced congratulations and caution from people I knew well and from those I had barely met. My reactions to other people's opinions depended on how deep I was in the Word, or how exhausted I was from striving in my own strength. I'll share two examples of these extremes. Let's start with the harder, weirder reaction first, like taking a band-aid off. After that, we'll at least have something to look forward to.

My husband and I were 11 months into the second adoption process. I had been given tickets to a Christian women's conference and invited a friend of mine to come with me. She was heavily pregnant and excited to have some girl time before motherhood came upon her. We met up, drove down, and immediately ran into a friend of a friend. One who didn't know that we BOTH were expecting. Let's call this friend Harriet.

Harriet walked up with a huge smile, "Oh my word, look at you about to pop. When are you due?" My friend grinned and gave all the salient details of her impending blessing.

Me: Sat there smiling awkwardly while being completely ignored. (It's fine. I'm fine.)

My Friend: "Oh, Jacqui is adopting." Attempting graciously to bring me into their conversation. (It had been ongoing for a while at this point while I watched the verbal tennis match.)

Harriet: "Oh...a baby? Why?"

.........Um...Yeah. So that happened. What began as a fun day with a friend, spending time in worship and in the Word, suddenly became a whole different 'thang.

Me, in my flesh: "What the What?!"

Me, actual words: "Yes. We're adopting a baby. We have our home study coming up soon. We're so excited."

Harriet: Blinks at me like a pigeon.

At that moment, I felt kind of crushed...like some of the shine was taken off my happiness. My mommy heart began arguing silently, "Why are you excited for her baby and not for mine? Why do you look uncomfortable? Why do I even want to justify this to you?"

I'm sure the singing, the testimonies, and the encouragement were great that day. I pretty much missed it as I struggled to reconcile what I had just experienced.

Here I was a mommy-to-be, just as much as my friend who was 145 months pregnant. Hers was to be a physical labor. But my labor, just as real, had been spiritual. And it had been years in the making. There was no epidural strong enough to alleviate the waves of pain and confusion I'd felt walking through this journey.

Here I was at a Christian women's event, surrounded by those who should know of God's heart for the fatherless, who should realize that

Jesus' earthly dad Joseph had essentially adopted him, and who should rejoice when families step out in faith. Harriet's silence was all it took to steal my joy in that moment. It was also what God used to underline for me how much of His church really doesn't get it.

Throughout scripture, God displays His heart for the orphan. He calls His people to stand in the gap, to defend the cause, to protect His kids, and to remember that true religion is to care for the orphan.

Actually, the very first book written in the Bible, Job, highlights a righteous man whom God had blessed abundantly. It is written that Job "rescued the fatherless" (Job 29:12).

Caring for the least of these is kind of the whole point of the Gospel. To my mind, there is no greater earthly example of salvation, God's adoption of us, than earthly fostering and adopting. So, to encourage those of you who have also come up against some Harriet-like comments and confusion, know that you are in good company. Remember that adoption was God's idea first. He's inviting you into His-story, and His story is always good.

The second example of, and much different response to, my sharing that I was adopting began when I was 27, childless, and coming to terms with another loss. A friend, let's call her Rosarita, mentioned to me that there was a young girl at a local university who was expecting. The mother was making an adoption plan.

At this point, after four miscarriages and a lifetime of knowing I was an adoptee, God shed light on His call on my life.

Me: "Oh, adoption. Yes, that's a great idea!"

No one has ever accused me of being super quick on the uptake. You read that correctly, it took me over a quarter of a century to recognize that God had kind of written adoption all over my life.

This particular birth mom and baby had a different path to take, but God used their story to bring to light parts of mine. Within 24 hours of having this conversation, I was headed to the airport to pick up my Momma and Grandma after a cruise vacation in Alaska.

They had been traveling for an entire day and were pretty much exhausted. I let none of their physical concerns slow me down. As I pulled up to the curb, I rolled down my window and pretty much yelled, "Guess what? We're gonna adopt!"

Curbside, amid the beeping of horns and the yelling of instructions, both their faces lit with joy and they started hollering back words of joy and excitement. Finally, I came to a full and complete stop, threw my door open, and we all hugged fiercely.

That evening, after spending a couple of hours talking about how this adoption would happen (collectively, with three generations of an adoptive Christian family plotting and planning, we had no actual clue what the next step was, but we were excited!), I called Rosarita.

> Rosarita: Quiet, and tired, "Hello?"
>
> Me: Again, completely unconcerned about anyone else's frame of mind in the face of my NEWS, "I'm gonna adopt!"
>
> Rosarita: "Oh, my word!" Within minutes, in her pajamas, Rosarita showed up at my door to hug me, celebrate, and reinstate the "How do you do this adoption thing?" conversation that I had engaged in earlier.

The fact that I had no agency, no baby-prospects, and pretty much no clue how the logistics of child placement worked did not stop me or my people from celebrating. God had shown up and shown us the way. I jumped into impending-motherhood eyes-wide shut, and for one of the first times in my life... jumped off a cliff trusting Father God to hold me tight. And He did.

I share these two differing reactions offered from different people to highlight that membership in a particular denomination, or even attendance at weekly Bible Study, doesn't mean that people will automatically "get it" when it comes to adoption and foster care. There are a lot of big feelings out there about what a "typical" family should look like. Depending on anyone's life experience and family of origin, they probably have some very real and visceral reactions to children and family alike.

I encourage you to surround yourself with cheerleaders. You need people who will encourage you in the good stuff and in the stuff that can feel kind of like garbage. The journey of parenthood is not for the faint of heart. When you walk into the spaces of child welfare to build a family, you are jumping into the deep end of the ocean. But guess what? The Guy who created the ocean also created that kid or those kiddos your heart already loves. His thoughts are higher than your thoughts, and this is all going to be for your good and for His glory. Hold on to those truths when the going feels rough, because Father God is walking this journey with you and will carry you when you feel slapped down and less shiny than you were ten minutes ago.

And let me be one of the first to congratulate you.

Me: "Oh My Word. Congratulations, you are going to be a parent! Booyah!"

Daddy's Take:

Over the course of our son's adoption, we both experienced the varied reactions that my wife listed above. Dads, note that it's highly probable that your wife's emotional response to the negative reactions will be different from yours. This is okay. Her experience coming into adoptive motherhood and your experience coming into adoptive fatherhood will be unique and personal to each of you.

Just remember to be present for her and to be processing your feelings as well. The best thing we did was keep praying together. A cord of three strands is not easily broken (Ecclesiastes 4:12).

Scripture for Your Journey:

Job 29:11–12
For those who heard me called me blessed, and those who saw me commended me, because I rescued the poor who cried out and the fatherless who had no helper.

Ecclesiastes 4:12
Though one may be overpowered, two can defend themselves. A cord of three strands is not quickly broken.

Zephaniah 3:17
The LORD your God is with you, he is mighty to save. He will take great delight in you, he will quiet you with his love, he will rejoice over you with singing.

Prayer for Your Journey:

Jesus,
As we say a holy Yes to the call to care for Your kid(s), we know that God is singing over us. Adoption is Your idea, and here on earth not everyone gets Your ideas immediately. We ask for a hedge of protection over our family, those who are here and those You will bring to us. We ask that You guard the hearts of the children who are waiting for parents to say "Yes." We pray for Your church to have revival in the area of child welfare so they will be the actual hands and feet of Jesus to those called into this journey. We ask that You help us shine up our joy when others' thoughtless words or reactions cause us pain. We know You are walking with us and we thank You for that. In Your holy name we pray, Amen.

Action Points:

1. Surround yourselves with those who will celebrate your Yes and will pray for you through the journey. Be diligent in seeking out those you can trust for discernment, ceaseless prayer, and joy!
2. When you are feeling tired, and possibly hopeless, reach out to these people for encouragement for them to fill you up with truth. Remember, with adoption, it isn't "if" it's when!
3. Be real and be prayerful. If some of your shine is stolen, remember the Captain of your team of supporters is the Author of Family, God Almighty. Bring it to Him, the hard stuff, the irritating stuff, and leave it at the cross. He can handle it.
4. Celebrate the milestones. You decided to adopt? Celebrate. You found an agency/ attorney etc.? Celebrate. You turned in the paperwork? CELEBRATE. Every child deserves to be celebrated, no matter what!

NOTES

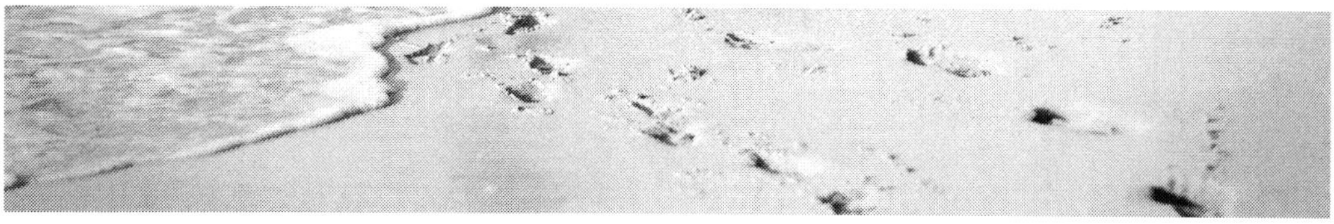

NOTES

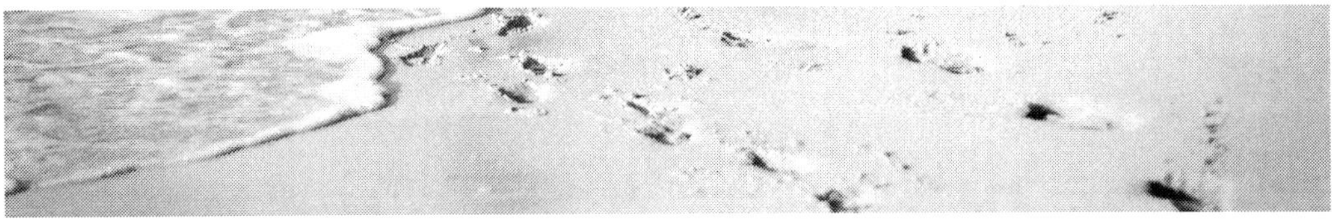

Chapter 8

WHO, WHERE, NOW WHAT?

Well, this is an exciting time for y'all. There is no telling where you are with your paperwork at this point. It is possible you are at the point of complete exhaustion. Good for you! You are moving into what I have always thought of as the second "try-mester," because truly this whole thing is just trying!

The exhaustion of the first segment is behind you. You have likely gathered enough documentation to form a paperwork trail of your entire life. If you have lived in many places, just getting the documentation on previous homes was likely a complicated and intricate process.

But you have persevered and now you are rewarded with a time of reprieve. I encourage you to look at it this way, because the alternative is what I did, and it just wasn't pretty.

Having asked God to help me move heaven and earth to get the paperwork done in record time, I suddenly hit a strange impasse. Even though I physically had little to do, I spiritually had plenty to do.

I had been fingerprinted and poked and prodded to the point that I was pretty sure I could run both criminal and medical tests on myself and others with relative ease from that point forward. I had coerced and begged family members and government gatekeepers alike to move our case quickly. I had flooded the FBI with (well-warranted, I might add) phone calls and even sent thank you notes. Now what? I had to face my spiritual nemesis: Patience...the Big "P."

In my heart, I had to understand that God is good all the time, and so is His timing. But after all the forward momentum, just waiting and wondering didn't feel very good. And that, friends, is when God did His best work in me. When I felt uncomfortable and needy, God moved. But this time, as in many times in my past, He didn't move in my circumstances; He moved in me. He taught me patience.

About the time that your paperwork is turned in, you will probably be notified that it is time for your home visit. This is the moment you have been working toward. Admittedly, this can be really scary. If you have ever seen any sitcom version of the Home Visit (I am thinking *Friends* circa November 13, 2003, not that I've watched it a million times or anything), it appears that everything that can go wrong actually does!

The first time I went through this rite of passage as a parent, I was thrilled. The house was decorated for Christmas, and I had cinnamon muffins baking in the oven. I was ready to pull out every trick in my arsenal and darn, but did my house smell good! The Christmas music was cued on the CD player, and crystal goblets and a carafe of water were perfectly positioned. I was ready to go, certain in my ignorance that at the completion of this interview I would be presented with a variety of beautiful babies just waiting to come home to Momma. It didn't quite happen that way, but what I did learn was that from this moment forward, the clock had started!

Here is something to encourage you as you let this truth settle in: The sooner you get your paperwork turned in and get placed on the home visit schedule, the sooner your adoption clock will start! From the time spanning from your initial decision to adopt to right now, you have had about as much control as you will have in this process. Enjoy it, revel in it, and then release it so that you are okay with being out of control.

The timeline of paperwork completion varies. For example, if you adopt through the state welfare service in some states, you will be required to take IMPACT or other such classes to become certified and approved as adoptive parents. These courses are offered on a predetermined timeline and may be as expedient as once a week or once a month. If you are adopting privately, there is a possibility of abbreviated paperwork as determined by your state, your attorney, and the birth mother's social service expectations. But as a good guideline, the home study is your ticket into the promised land of patience.

I often pray for peace, not patience, because I know my Jesus! If I ask Him for growth in a spiritual area, He will oblige, and the only way to get patience is to have things I have to wait for. So, as you walk toward this total adoption milestone, know that you are walking into a divinely gray area, and that is just fine. You may not be able to see the entire pathway, but God will light each step in front of you as you learn to lean on Him. Surrender is beautiful, but it is not easy; however, day by day, breath by breath, just remember you are one step closer to your child, and that is a wonderful thing.

Daddy's Take:

My wife and I wait differently. Whereas I was hopeful, but not laser-focused on the pending adoption; she was honed in on a target. Note that that does not mean I loved our child-to-be any less than she did; I just processed it differently. My wife was focused on the miraculous. And miraculous it was. When the obstacles to our son's adoption began to resolve, I knew in my heart that it was directly related to the prayers, tears, and patience of my wife. I was and remain so grateful to have witnessed the miracle and to be able to tell our boy how much we both loved him, but also how very hard my wife fought for him in prayer. It wasn't easy, but it was worth it.

Scripture for Your Journey:

Romans 12:12
Be joyful in hope, patient in affliction, faithful in prayer.

Philippians 4:6–7
6 *Do not be anxious about anything, but in every situation, by prayer and*
petition, with thanksgiving, present your requests to God. 7 *And the peace*
of God, which transcends all understanding, will guard your hearts and
your minds in Christ Jesus.

Prayer for Your Journey:

Dear Lord,
There is so very little that we can control in life. This remains true for the adoption of our child. We have done what we can. We have prayed over paperwork, interviews, and documentation. Now we have to release it. That idea of surrender in favor of patience is not easy, but please help us to cling to this truth. It is sweet to surrender to a God we know loves us so deeply and loves our child-to-be just as much. Hold us now, Lord. Amen.

Action Points:

1. What questions do you specifically have for the social worker or attorney as you reach this milestone?
2. Which part of this process right now is hardest for you to release and surrender?
3. Have you checked with the agency, attorney, or other point-person to make sure all the paperwork is complete, accurate, and being processed? Don't just assume it is being processed. As part of your due diligence, it will be important to follow up.
4. Feel free to ask for timelines, but be sure to surrender these to God.

NOTES

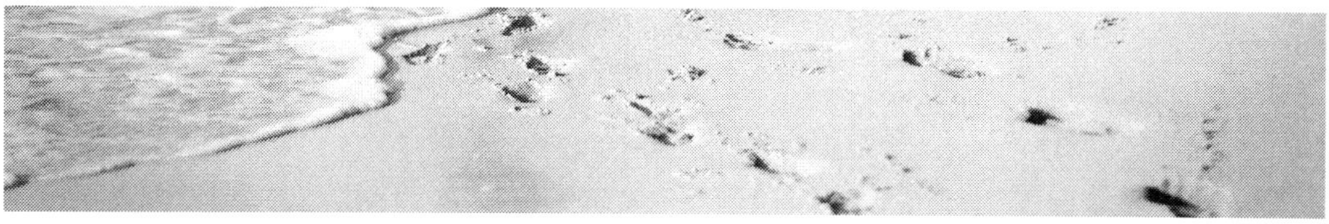

NOTES

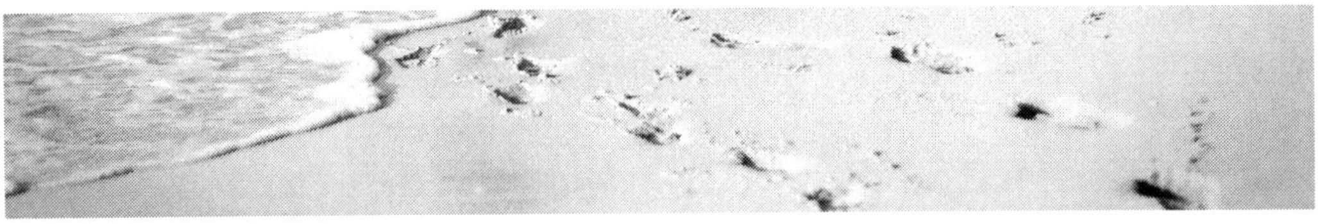

Chapter 9

THE SPIRITUAL OPPOSITION TO ADOPTION

It is important to realize that those who adopt may face spiritual warfare during their adoption journey. However, it is highly unlikely that you will be able to know if the obstacles you are facing are the result of a fallen world or a direct spiritual attack. When multiple obstacles hit back to back, does the cause really matter? What matters is that you are in a pit and need peace. Sweet friend, please hear me as I say this: The important thing is not to ascertain the exact impetus of the battles you have hit, but rather to keep your faith strong in the midst of these trials.

Your job is to pray for God's peace, provision, and timing, knowing that He has the final word on all of this. When you take your focus off of the label and put it firmly on the solution, it reorients your perspective in a positive way. You have a choice between two options: to spin your wheels fretting or to pray in faith. This being said, it's important to discuss the spiritual warfare element since it actually is a factor. As an adoptee, and as adoptive momma, I do believe that the Modern Orphan is spiritually opposed, but I also know the most important truth: God's got this! So here we go!

Wouldn't it be lovely if all those sweet little ones awaiting a forever family and all those parents-in-waiting could simply find one another quickly? Christian Alliance for Orphans (CAFO) maintains that while 33% of Americans consider adoption, only 2% complete the process. This is heartbreaking. Families may be physically exhausted and financially spent after invasive infertility treatments. They may have a child or two at home and feel overwhelmed by the costs associated with a typical adoption. It feels hopeless, and this hopeless place is exactly where the enemy wants us.

Families grieve a child they've never held. Children grieve the parents they have yet to find. Satan is laughing at us as we try to consider our next step. Orphans, both globally and locally, can be attacked from the womb. Satan has an arsenal at his disposal including war, disease, poverty, addiction, and all manner of brokenness. Take heart, though, for Psalm 34:18 states, "The Lord is close to the brokenhearted."

We raise empty arms heavenward and scream, "Why is this so hard? Why isn't our child home yet?"

As obstacles mount, you hear the enemy's lies saying that you aren't meant to adopt. The process is too hard, the bureaucracy is too much, the paperwork is too foreboding, the cost is too high. Please, please stay connected to the God who loves you, and the people who are walking through this with you. Satan's goal is to "kill and steal and destroy," but Jesus came so that we "may have life, and have it to the full" (John 10:10).

I've met so many sweet families desiring a child who month by month invested in medicine to bring about a miracle until a well-meaning physician finally prescribed adoption as a poor second choice to a biological birth. This causes many hopeful Christian parents-to-be to walk up to an adoption process with apprehension instead of hope.

Many families who have endured grieving the loss of a child, whether through a miscarriage or different occurrence, come out the other side bruised. However, by God's grace, these families can also come out stronger and more focused. These families can be the ones God specifically calls to adopt, for they have been to the school of suffering and have been trained in patience and know how to wait in the moments when the future is unknown. Adoption is akin to a marathon, and as all athletes know, strength comes from training and hard work.

Take heart! Every orphan is spoken for by Jesus, and every child is precious to Him. God is in the business of forming families, but we must remember we have a very real enemy working to destroy all God loves.

Okay, enough thinking about the hard stuff, now focus on the God who is greater and bigger and loves you and your child dearly. Focus on truth as you prepare to walk further into this amazing love story the Father is writing just for you!

Daddy's Take:

I'm a disabled veteran. I've been sent into war zones, and I've experienced combat training missions. War is good preparation for an adoption journey. I'm serious. You have to surrender fully to the One, the only One, who is in command. You have to have total faith that the steps of obedience you are asked to take will protect those you've sworn to protect. You have to know in the core of your being that you are fighting for something bigger than you. Do what comes naturally to every soldier regardless of creed, color, or religion when fear strikes: Hit your knees, and pray like crazy.

Scripture for Your Journey:

Lamentations 3:22–23
[2]*Because of the Lord's great love we are not consumed,*
for his compassions never fail.
They are new every morning;
great is your faithfulness.

John 16:33
In this world you will have trouble. But take heart! I have overcome the world.

Exodus 14:14
The Lord will fight for you; you need only to be still.

Prayer for Your Journey:

Dear Jesus,
We recognize that the battle is real. We recognize that You are greater than any obstacle we hit. But as we walk this journey, we ask for You to hold us tight. We ask that You send the resources, support, and encouragement we will desperately need, and we ask that these needs are met exactly when they need to be. We trust You, God, on behalf of our hearts and on behalf of the child we wait to meet, love, and welcome home forever. Amen.

Action Points:

1. What do you need from your community to make this calling a reality?

2. Some well-meaning people may present adoption as a second choice. How can you respond in love, while holding true to God's heart for the orphan?
3. Share and pray over the greatest obstacles and challenges you have faced and overcome so far. Note God's faithfulness during this process in the big and in the little.

NOTES

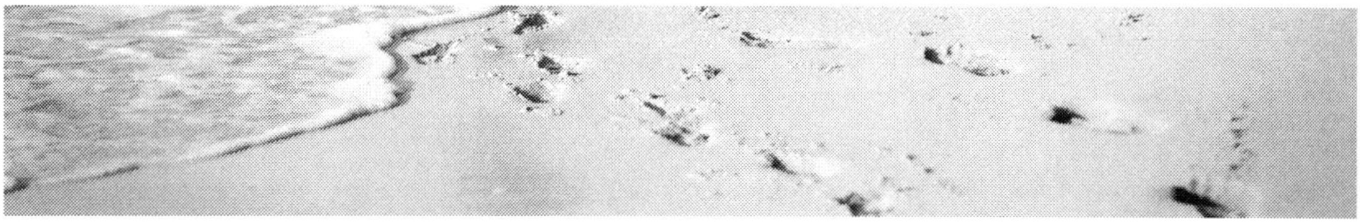

NOTES

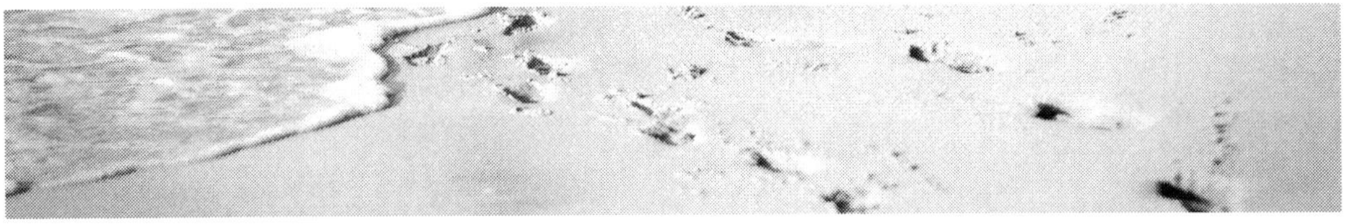

Chapter 10

MOVING OUT OF THE DARKNESS

In the last chapter, I may have sounded like your bossy older sister. If so, I am so sorry! Obstacles are a real part of all this, but this is not where I (or, more importantly, God) want you to focus. It was hard for me to write about, because it was overwhelming for me to live through. You have likely faced a lot in your adoption journey as well. Take this as encouragement: Satan wouldn't bother messing with you if you weren't on the right path!

Simply take a moment and just breathe. Stop and grieve if that is how you feel. It is critical that you, your spouse, and your family communicate openly about where you have been and where you are going. Please ask God for spiritual healing and release from the hard stuff. I know you don't want to use this journey to fill a God-sized hole with a child-sized soul. Disappointment will surely follow if this happens.

So, push pause if you have to. Regroup in community and in your family, and ask God to move you forward when the time is right. I say this because I am one of His more stubborn children, and I routinely have to be pushed like a donkey to move on.

I remember the state of my heart after enduring an invasive medical procedure and two rounds of hormone treatment. I had a well-meaning infertility doctor call me into his office to gently say, "Jacqui, take some time off from 'trying' and talk with someone." That poor man. I still need to send an apology.

I fell to absolute pieces and started weeping copiously. How dare he, a father already, look at me and tell me to stop treatment in favor of counseling. I wasn't getting any younger! At the ripe old age of 28, I had several friends working on babies number two and three in their families, and my biological clock had been ringing at high alert levels for years. But alas, I acquiesced. During this meeting, I found out that my chances of conceiving and carrying were less than 2%. I did what anybody would do with a heart crisis: I had myself a good old-fashioned ugly cry.

I'm so thankful that Jesus did not leave me there in my brokenness and longing. I had a dear friend, my shepherding deacon from church, who had also walked a difficult journey to motherhood. She phoned me with a divinely-timed message that same week. She spoke with wisdom, saying, "Jacqui, you are hurt and in need of healing. You are mad at God, and I get it. But whatever you do, do not stop talking to God!" This may seem like fairly obvious advice, but it can also be extremely frustrating. Track with me here for a minute.

In our most broken moments, pulling away from a God who is allowing the hurt seems like a go-to reaction as a self-preservation mechanism. I have sadly watched many friends or loved ones face a season of pain and pull away from truth, community, and, ultimately, the God who loves them. If you throw hormones, emotional heartache, and finances into the mix, it can get nasty very fast. My friend's advice to me was spot on. I had only been processing for a few days and could have easily made some self-destructive choices. I felt extremely beaten down.

Just as King David of the Psalms had to yell and cry out to God, so can we! God knows it all anyways; our hurt is not a surprise to Him. He knows every facet of your feelings, experiences, and how very much you may just want the season to end. Be real with Him. God knows all of you, and He can see behind the fake smiles and the "I'm fine!"s. He is there waiting to comfort and care for you.

When my friend told me to be honest with God, I began to stomp, yell, and question Him in a way that would have made King David blush. But God just sat with me, lovingly waiting out my full-blown temper tantrum. And when I was spent, God held me. He held me in His loving arms. He held me together.

After all that drama, I chose to hit pause. I had to lean into Jesus in a real way. It wasn't easy, and it wasn't my first choice, but it was my best choice. I was able to grieve this impossible place I found myself in, and God began a work in me that ultimately led me to find my first child. The promise of tomorrow is what I had to cling to through this difficult time.

Once that process had played itself out, I had to make a decision: Should I trust God and move forward or trust myself and stay stagnant? Because of the prayers of many and the sweet words of my friend who understood, I had the courage to move forward, and I am so grateful that I did. I felt ready to begin anew. I was safe in His dream for me and released from mine. And let's face it—God's dreams for us are always infinitely more exciting, thrilling, and fulfilling than our own dreams.

Daddy's Take:

The emotional toll that the adoption process can take may manifest differently in women than in men, but when you are one in marriage, you will also experience your spouse's pain and confusion. Men, if your wife is heartbroken and struggling, this is your chance to be the hands and feet of Jesus to her hurting heart. Satan wants to use this time to break you both down, but it can become a time of intimacy between you and your wife.

Scripture for Your Journey:

1 Thessalonians 5:8
But since we belong to the day, let us be sober, putting on faith and love as a breastplate, and the hope of salvation as a helmet.

2 Chronicles 20:17
You will not have to fight this battle. Take up your positions; stand firm and see the deliverance the Lord will give you, Judah and Jerusalem. Do not be afraid; do not be discouraged. Go out to face them tomorrow, and the Lord will be with you.

Prayer for Your Journey:

Dear Jesus,
This season feels unending. It feels so hard, and truly, it feels unfair. Why are You allowing this? Right now, that is all I can ask. Why? But God, You are a Good Father. You really are. I want to be a good parent like You. Please God, speak truth to me. If You have called me to this journey, I trust that this time of waiting and wondering is not meant as a punishment but as a preparation for the joys and even the trials of parenting. Lord, You have put that desire into my heart, so even as I am bruised and broken, I

know You see me. I know You hear me. And I claim that there is purpose in all of this. I pray You bring peace. And I pray You move quickly to help us find the child You have for us. Though we have never seen this child with our own eyes or held this child with our own arms, we know You are in control. Thank You for that. Amen.

Action Points:

1. How is your heart? Check in with each other from time to time. Remember that to wage this battle to find your family, you'll both need to be solid in your connection to Jesus and to one another.
2. Are there any dreams that you still have not released?
3. What obstacles have you faced since the beginning of your journey? List all these obstacles. Some common obstacles are as follows: 1. lack of family support, 2. finances, or 3. locating an agency or social worker. As you list these battles, also give yourself space to write the date and specific way that God answered these issues. Seeing His faithfulness and actually writing down the ways God has handled your situations will give you encouragement that He is there fighting for you now, whether you see and feel it or not.
4. *If you need to pause in this process to work through grief or transition with a clergy member, counselor, or community, please take time to do so. It will be healthier for your child if you handle it now.*

NOTES

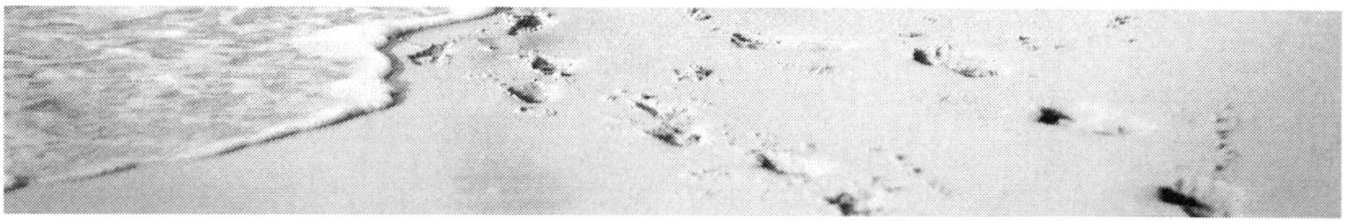

NOTES

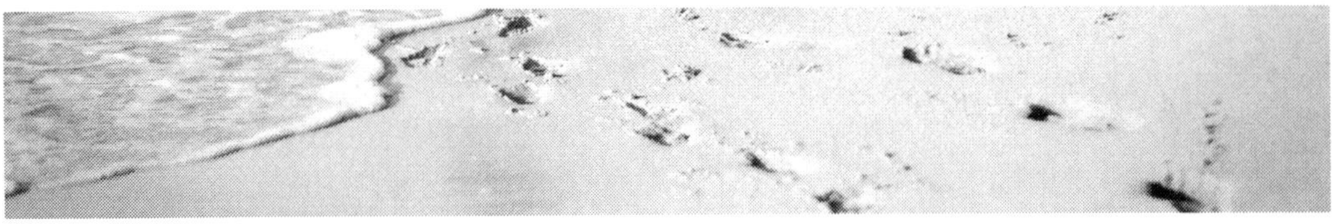

Chapter 11

HURRY UP AND WAIT!

The Hubs is former military, and he compares the adoption process to battle. Prepare, prepare, prepare, and then hurry up and wait. You've done your part. You've researched agency options, prayed it up and down, and discussed adoption with family and friends!

The flurry of activity that comes once an adoption course is set could be comical if it wasn't so incredibly draining. From my own adoption from Colombia, I still have a binder that is at least three inches thick that has survived over 30 years. My two oldest children will each be recipients of their own adoption binders, approximately four inches thick and full of blood, sweat, and tears that show the effort we took in becoming a family.

And then came the lull, the weird waiting period. It's that strange calm before the storm that precedes the next flurry of activity that brings your child home. The hardest thing for me about that lull is that I don't always know long the wait is going to take.

If you are adopting internationally, you may be given a timeline and possibly even wait times until you are matched. If you are adopting domestically, these timelines are thin on the ground. They can possibly give you statistics from previous years, but given the newer focus on open adoptions, birth parents often choose their forever families. This is a great boon to your child, and can be one for your entire family, but this is where trust in God becomes your lifeline.

During the adoption of our second child, we flew through the initial paperwork and interviews in record time. I was convinced that we were in God's timing, which we were, but I misinterpreted that to mean that the adoption would happen both easily and quickly, which it didn't.

As I mentioned in the previous chapters, we hit obstacles. What I pray you find from my personal anecdotes is that obstacles are just opportunities for God to show up. In my overexcitement and in my mommy heart, I felt each obstacle as a brick crushing my dreams and making me yet again question my faith. I'm not some amazing faith-filled person; I'm just one girl who walked this adoption road in a variety of ways and lived to tell the tale.

When my husband and I were initially approved as prospective parents, we shared the happy news far and wide. We bought bibs that said, "I love Daddy!" and "I love Mommy!" We announced it at a dinner with family and friends. We all but wrote it in the sky. Then the agency called...three times in a row. We weren't at that "waiting for a phone call" stage, so my oversensitive mommy antennae didn't take the calls as happy signs. The voicemails sounded worse, and I waited with bated breath for the Hubs to get home so we could return the calls together.

Our agency worker's husband transferred to another state for his job. Her last day was the end of that very week. As the last couple approved in that calendar year, we would be the last couple to continue on with our paperwork journey once they found a replacement, trained the social worker, and then had that new worker meet with every other prospective family who had been ahead of us. Our timeline was completely interrupted. We had to push pause from December through July.

Oh my gracious, y'all! There I was again at the push-pause phase. Righteously indignant, I felt justified in telling anyone who would hang around long enough to listen to my well-rehearsed diatribe that this was repugnant. My child might be in the world right now! Pausing would make him or her wait for Mommy and Daddy, and that was unconscionable. I felt like the rug was pulled out from under me. Sadly, it never once crossed my mind that the other 23 families who were working with that same agency got similar calls.

To be completely honest, I was so upset that I looked at the Hubs and demanded that he call the agency and pull our profile. I didn't want to do the dirty work myself, but I was happy to pawn it off on him. The idea wasn't well-thought-out or prayed over, but in that particular moment I felt defeated, and in my defeat, I fell into my flesh. My heart focused on my personal pain.

At that moment, God showed up audibly, which has only happened to me a handful of times in my years as a believer. I heard out loud, "Be still and know that I am God" (Psalm 46:10). I remember hearing it distinctly as I was driving with my three-year-old daughter in her car seat behind me. I actually turned around, wondering at her ventriloquism abilities, when I realized, "Nope that was God, and He sees me about to lose it."

So, I parked the car and prayed out loud while sitting in the front seat. My preschooler, the sweet little love that she is, folded her hands and prayed along with me. Whereas my amen sounded exhausted and heavy, hers sounded firm and enthusiastic. She knew I was praying for "our baby" as she called it, but she did so with joy. That was a total lesson for this mommy.

I had some choices to make. Would I choose bitterness and risk missing the joy and goodness that God really did have for me during the wait, or would I choose joy and find hope in the wait? Thankfully, although I didn't always get it right, I chose joy the majority of the time during this season.

Jeff and I were trying to figure out our finances, as we knew this adoption would be much more expensive than the previous one. I took to rambling around our home looking at furniture (We don't really need that many chairs!) and décor (We don't need more than one lamp; we can use candles!). I jumped into a Craig's-list craze with reckless abandon. My thought was to sell all the excess and put that money towards the adoption. I even began to run again; this was a pastime I had used to get "wedding-ready" earlier, but it now became my prayer time. I'd run for miles, dedicating each mile to a different aspect of our adoption: our paperwork, our interviews, our wait, our birth family, and our child.

As the list got longer, the miles grew too. Finally, I realized I could put all the running to good use. We sent letters to family and friends to sponsor me in the Disney Princess Half Marathon in Orlando. I was running in honor and support of adoption.

The training grew more intense, and I enlisted a friend to run with me for encouragement and support. The weekend of the race expo, our little family of three drove down to Florida and shared our dreams with Mickey and his friends. True to the "dreams come true" spirit of the event, Disney cast members gave our little girl a "Big Sister" button, and Jeff and I sported buttons with all the Disney Characters that said, "Ask us about our adoption!" I made a purple t-shirt that had Romans 3:23 written on the back and told the world I was running in honor of Baby Nehi. (Nehemiah was the prayer name we used to refer to our baby.) Needless to say, God used the run and the wait by allowing us to share our journey with others in a pretty cool way.

I share the specifics of the where and the when because again God spoke. Reflecting on this, I am recognizing the truth that perhaps when we are in the center of God's will, we are able to hear our Father a little more clearly. As I ran down Main Street in Disney World, the sun began to peek over Cinderella's Castle, and I began to bawl. Onlookers at 6 am were cheering us runners along. The cool January air was giving way to a muggy and potentially warm morning, and I was about halfway through my race. All of this heightened my senses and increased my speed, but what really floored me was the spiritual aspect.

I had been praying for six miles over our adoption, and it was like God just came over me, or in a sense, overshadowed me. I felt His presence as clearly as I feel my own children when I hold them. I knew to my core that something was moving in the heavenly realm, something that completely impacted the adoption process. It was confirmation of the clearest kind that we were in His will, and that although it was unseen by me, He was directing our path. At that moment, with my heart full to overflowing, I knew I was God's Princess. I was dearly loved and directed. It was humbling.

As I shared, I am not a world-class athlete looking to set a personal record with every race. In fact, this race had multiple opportunities for photo ops with characters and Disney icons. Up to this point, I had ignored the hoopla, but this feeling was too important not to document. As I ran over the bridge and inside the castle I spotted some photographers. I got in line, still pumping my legs, and yes, still bawling, and got a picture. I knew this was a big moment for my family, but I just didn't know why...yet.

Daddy's Take:

I remember watching Jacqui cross the finish line at the Princess race. This was not her first half, but it is the one I remember most clearly because of the emotion on her face. She later told me what she had experienced, what she knew deep in her heart.

Trying to maintain a firm "let's not get ahead of ourselves" response, I very gently reminded her that the agency had given us a two-year timeline once we were approved for home study. We were nowhere close to this timeline; we were in the pause phase. She was insistent though, and with the benefit of hindsight, I now know conclusively that our Father spoke words of peace and encouragement to my wife's heart during that prayer run. I know that as my wife ran her heart out for our baby boy, the wheels in heaven were indeed moving.

Scripture for Your Journey:

Ecclesiastes 3:1
For everything there is a season, and a time for every matter under heaven...

2 Corinthians 10:5
We destroy arguments and every lofty opinion raised against the knowledge of God, and take every thought captive to obey Christ....

Prayer for Your Journey:

Dear Lord,
The obstacles are real. These things make us wonder if we are on the right path or even in Your will at all. Jesus, help us to take every concern, every conflicting emotion, and every thought to You. Help us to remember that You are a Good Father, and that You have the perfect plan and season for all that is to come. Let us lean into You when we don't understand the wait, knowing that You do. Most of all, don't let us waste this time. Let us fill it up with You. Amen.

Action Points:

1. During the wait, what will help you stay connected to each other and to God?
2. What are some personal examples of you waiting for something long-desired very patiently? When did you not do so well?
3. Journal some Scriptural encouragement to post conspicuously in your home or your vehicle that will help you hear truth during the wait.
4. Share with your family/community about how they can support you during the wait.

NOTES

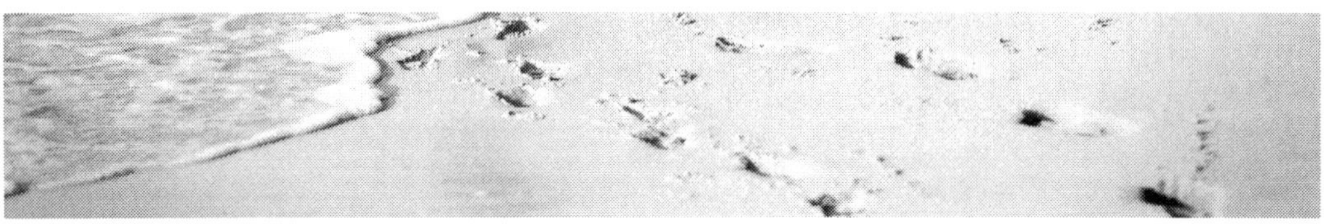

NOTES

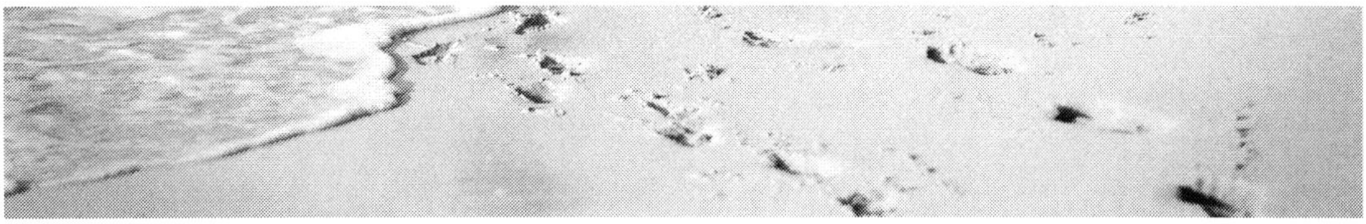

Chapter 12

HOW TO PRAY DURING THE WAIT

As I mentioned before, some of you may blow through the adoption journey at supersonic speed. I love that for y'all, and I honestly pray that for each of you. Statistically, many of us will be paper pregnant without a due date for what feels like far too long. Remember, you have the spiritual aspect you may contend with, but there is also the human aspect of bureaucracy and unending paperwork that can all combine to make this feel like an unending season.

So, what should you do? During seasons of waiting, of which I believe I have somehow experienced more than the average girl's share, I have found that God is there ready to teach me something. Apparently, I have a lot to learn. One thing that has been made clear to me is that God will use anything to get me to dig deeper into my relationship with Him. During some seasons, He has had to endure me kicking and screaming until I wore myself out; then, and only then, was the deepening and depending able to begin. In our current season of growth, the Hubs and I have a new prayer that I will share with you.

It typically goes something like this:

> Dear Jesus, meet us where we are right now. We thank You for loving us. Our feelings aren't fact, but we are bogged down in our circumstances. Jesus, give us teachable and humble spirits so that we can learn whatever You want to teach us quickly. We don't want to waste time wandering in the desert. We trust You and love You, and we know You love us and our family. Help us to rest in that truth and in your love. Amen and Amen.

We have a combined total of about 80 years' worth of experience kicking and fighting before finally realizing that—yes!—God is good all the time, and we want to go straight to "Thy will" and not "my will." This was a hard transition for me, folks. My husband has a much more humble spirit than I do, and depending on God through prayer helped mold a more humble spirit within me. One part of my brokenness was the wait to get our family home safe, but I know I am a more prayerful momma because of it. Was the trade-off worth it? Absolutely!

I had to learn how to journal. For me, the written word is soothing and solidifying. Simply being able to write things out takes my jumbled heart-mess and removes the toxic from deep within. Some of these journals, quite honestly, will need to be burned before anyone finds them, but it is a true reflection of exactly where my heart was in a given season.

Journaling also gave me the opportunity to reflect once an answer came. I had dates and times listed, and regardless of whether the answer came fairly quickly or after years of prayer and petition, every single prayer was answered. There is a caveat—the answers weren't always the ones I was hoping for. Sometimes the answer was to pray more, without ceasing. Sometimes the answer was to wait—(GRRR!—more growth!), and sometimes the answer was a startling, "No!" But even the answers I didn't want gave clarity and peace to my heart when I recognized that the prayers of an open heart will be answered, and that answer is always God's best.

I had to realize all this as a sweaty, tired, and very emotional runner: God's right there wiping away the tears, crying alongside me, and waiting for that perfect moment when He moves mountains and boom—answers abound!

Praying is truly the key. There's nothing magical about prayer; it just gets us into the mindset and the heartset, if you will, to really hear from the Father who loves us, who is there cheering us on as we run this race. This is not to say that prayer isn't powerful and doesn't move mountains, for it does. It's just that when you have the opportunity to wait—oh this is so hard even mentioning, but it's still true!—when you have the opportunity to wait, don't waste it. Turn all those cares into prayers and watch how God holds you through it all.

Daddy's Take:

My wife is a five-foot-tall prayer warrior. She prays more than any person I've ever known, and she sees those prayers answered more than anyone

I've ever met. But this has been an area in which I've watched her stretch and grow over the years. And all of her growth encouraged me to grow, too. We are both ready to hit our knees whenever obstacles hit, which they will, for we've seen the faithfulness of God in our lives. And you will, too.

Scripture for Your Journey:

Psalm 27:14
Wait for the Lord;
be strong, and let your heart take courage;
wait for the Lord!

Galatians 6:9
And let us not grow weary of doing good, for in due season we will reap, if we do not give up.

Prayer for Your Journey:

Dear Jesus,
Don't let us waste the wait. We want to bring all our cares to the foot of the cross, and we will make time to do it. We love You, and You love those whom we love. You wait for us, just as we wait for this child. Jesus, help us to grow in our communion and relationship with You, so that all of the children You ask us to steward will be blessed and encouraged by the example we set. Amen.

Action Points:

1. What excites you or scares you about the wait?
2. How do you think your spouse perceives this time of waiting?
3. Is there anything at all that you want to share with your Heavenly Father? (He knows it all, but He's a gentleman, so He won't push His way into your life. He will wait for you to share with Him!)
4. What are a couple of specific prayer requests that you'd like your prayer team or small group to pray for you during this time?

NOTES

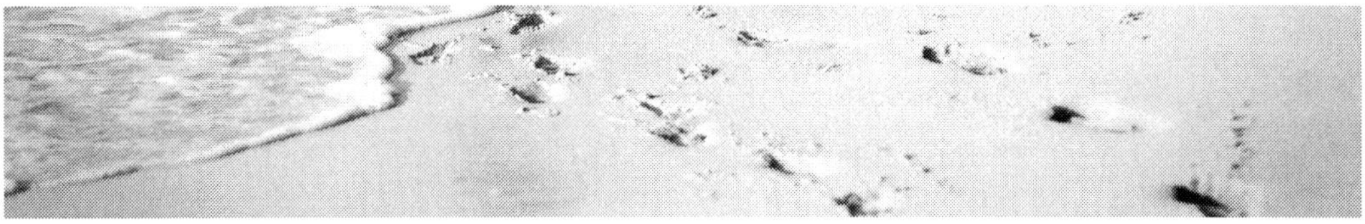

NOTES

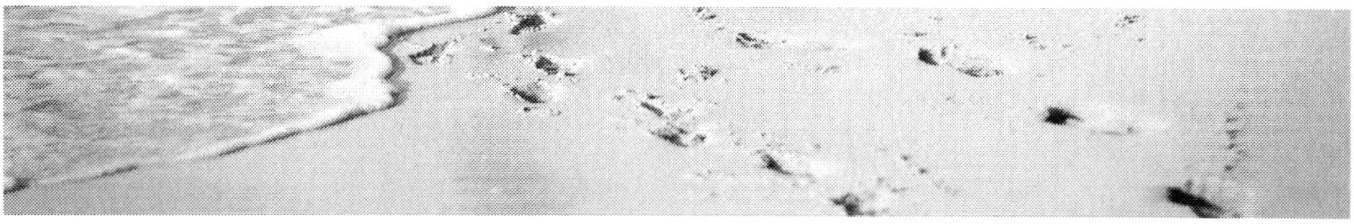

Chapter 13

HOW TO RELY ON GODLY COUNSEL

If you haven't completed this next step already, soon you will have to narrow your focus down to adopting domestically or internationally. You will also have to consider whether you want to adopt through foster care or not. This will be imperative, for each of these decisions moves you closer to finding your child. Here is a little secret about adoption that just doesn't pertain to a biological addition: You will likely have scant information about things you need to know, and you will have too much information about things you don't need to know. What's a momma and daddy to do? First, you have got to be prayerful and in the Word, both individually and collectively. I say this because, in order for you to discern God's will for your life, and more specifically, for your adoption, you have to be able to hear Him. To know Him is to listen and to listen is to be in the Word. Stay prayerful and stay surrounded by Godly counsel.

As you enter into this next phase of your adoption journey, identify friends, another couple, or clergy members who are committed to praying alongside you and your family. These people will ideally have experience with adoption in some form; however, God can use anyone. If the people whom you identify or who volunteer are people you would go to for spiritual guidance in other areas, then bingo! They will be worth their weight in gold by the end of this journey.

Exodus 17:11–12 states, "As long as Moses held up his hands, the Israelites were winning, but whenever he lowered his hands, the Amalekites were winning. When Moses' hands grew tired, they took a stone and put it under him and he sat on it. Aaron and Hur held his hands up—one on one side, one on the other—so that his hands remained steady till sunset." When you are depleted, defeated, and down, your Godly counsel will be your Aaron and Hur by holding your arms up, encouraging you to fight on, and giving you much-needed support and encouragement. The importance of these people cannot be overstated. Adoptions can be lengthy and confusing, but just think of the journey as if it is a master's course in parenting, for parenting will have complicated elements as well. Just as biological parents have a team around them supporting their maternity period, you also should have a team built of prayer warriors and encouragers who are willing to stand in the gap for your family and give possibly hard to hear but desperately needed counsel.

About ten years ago, I sat in my dear friend Brittany's home as she shared life-changing information about a baby-to-be who would need a forever home. This came on the heels of much soul-searching, prayer, and several months of invasive and ineffective infertility treatment. I had found myself at a crossroads, but thankfully my parents had walked a similar journey and knew the answer—to pray. The pastor had even come over for lunch and prayed over my broken mommy heart. God caught me off guard by using this sweet friend as an answer to years of prayer as she shared words of hope regarding adoption. Those words completely changed the course for this entire family. Interestingly, that sweet baby she mentioned was never released for adoption; however, that little soul has had a significant impact on our family's heart, our family's unique design, and on this ministry, and it is solely because of the prayers of many.

About four years ago, we were entering another adoption process. I enthusiastically and stubbornly insisted on returning to the same agency even though this new adoption would take place in a different state. I was way too hesitant to step outside of the known. Every step of the way we hit obstacles, which I still maintain is pretty much par for the course when Christians step out in faith to adopt God's children. I started to think differently about using the same agency: Maybe we were supposed to adopt another way. I also kept hearing from friends providing Godly counsel. They kept saying that we needed to consider broadening our search and to be prepared to move quickly when the time came.

That surprised and irritated me. I had a plan I was comfortable with, so I thought, "Back off, people!" But the constant wave of truth continued unabated, regardless of my comfort level. Looking back, I realize now that people who loved us, who loved our child-to-be, and who knew and heeded God's Word were attempting to share what God was telling them. I had to be in the right place with Jesus to really hear them. As the wheels in heaven began to turn, God used pretty much everything in His power to level me, including three weeks of bedrest after a minor outpatient surgery. I relented, and suddenly everything regarding the adoption started to move at supersonic speed.

Please hear me when I say that if I had to guess, I believe the obstacles we faced were spiritual in nature. As stated in previous chapters, we have a real enemy who does not want children placed in Godly homes. Our children-to-be are banking on us pushing through for them. We began prayerfully, continued through the journey prayerfully, and finally closed out our son's adoption very prayerfully. However, I'm here to tell you that even God's prayerful and faithful have moments of desperation, confusion, and the tendency toward comfort in the midst of the unknown. That's what God was working on in my heart.

My daughter's adoption and my own adoption were pretty much textbook as far as timelines, paperwork, and completion. Although at times these journeys felt perilous, cumbersome, and unending, they went more smoothly than many other adoption stories. My sister's adoption and my son's adoption could not have had more left turns! Although I wanted to cling to comfort, God took me out of that box and moved the Hubs and me to where we needed to be to find our son and bring him home safely.

Leaving the known and jumping head first into the unknown is likely very scary for you, too. For me, the need for wise and Godly counsel could not have been more important in these instances. As I mentioned before, there were honestly times when I was so overwhelmed that I would look at my dear husband and demand that he call the agency and pull us out of the adoption process. I wouldn't do the dirty deed, but I was not above fit-throwing to have him do it. Thankfully, he is not only more pragmatic than I am, but also more willing to be still and listen. He would look right at me and say, "Jacqui, God isn't telling us to quit." At those moments when my heart was terribly beaten down and my spirit was crying out, all of our Godly counsel was praying us on. I knew our adoption team was banging on heaven's gates for the life of our young child.

Daddy's Take:

The wait was hard. Because of how my wife and I process differently, it was harder for her, and that left me feeling helpless. All I could do was pray for her. I prayed for God to give us both peace and to listen to the prayer warriors He had put in our lives "for such a time as this" (Esther 4:14). If you are completing an adoption, that is most certainly the time to be in community. It is the time to be authentic about your prayer needs. You need time to be honest with your Godly counsel, but then let God be Lord of your family.

Scripture for Your Journey:

Psalm 46:10
Be still, and know that I am God.
I will be exalted among the nations,
I will be exalted in the earth!

Esther 4:14
...who knows whether you have not come to the kingdom for such a time as this?

Prayer for Your Journey:

Jesus,
Thank You for our adoption team. Thank You for their prayerfulness, nearness to our hearts, and willingness to speak truth. Even if their words may be hard to hear at times, we thank You because through their strength, we can gather our strength and press on. This journey can make us feel so weary, but Lord, we know that in the perfect time, You will take all that pain, waiting, and wanting and replace it with the most amazing gift: the gift of family. Thank You, God! Amen.

Action Points:

1. What areas are the hardest for you as you endure the wait?

What areas do you want or need your prayer team to focus on specifically? Examples may be: for the government to move quickly on adoption requests, exit visas, and paperwork; for the birth mother's emotions and health; for the home study to be filled out completely and accurately; or for any complicated visa paperwork to be completed well and accepted quickly.

2. In what areas are you feeling weak? Be honest because Jesus already knows, and it will help everyone to know how to support you.

NOTES

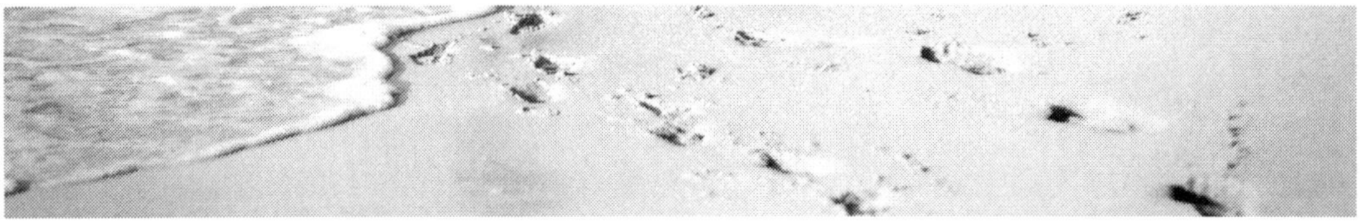

NOTES

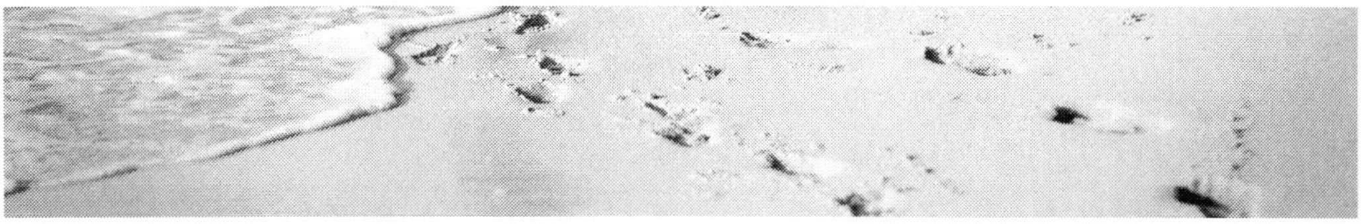

Chapter 14

INFORMATION OVERLOAD

The last several chapters have dealt specifically with spiritual warfare, the need for prayer, and the need for Godly counsel. Here is where the rubber meets the road. The old adage that states, "It takes a village to raise a child" can be changed to state, "It takes a village to adopt a child." You have to have social workers, agency workers, at least one government, and at least one judge finally says, "Yep, that's your child." Having that many different people and institutions agree on this one overarching goal takes a literal act of Congress and several acts of God.

But there's another aspect to this support team that may need more than a cursory glance: your child's therapist. From what I have observed, it is likely that your child may have some extra special areas that need to be addressed. Please sweet friend, keep reading. If you are already open and willing to consider or even embrace some special needs, then God bless you, truly! He will fully lead you. These are His children, and He has hand-picked you! However, maybe you are more like I was in this season: holding tightly to a dream and very unwilling to release "my will" to "Thy will" in this area. So here we go!

In today's world, the introduction of technology has completely changed the way that medical, social, and cognitive diagnoses are considered, shared, or reviewed during an adoption. Sometimes this is a huge benefit, for parents can prepare ahead of time for possible needs. This can allow families to recruit support people in their area to give therapy or treatment as needed once placement has occurred. Googling needed information takes less time than ordering a chicken sandwich at the drive thru. However, sometimes the information provided is skeletal at best. Having to wait days, weeks, and possibly months for answers to understandably reasonable and pertinent questions about your child's physical and mental health can feel like agony.

This is where discernment, wisdom, and your prayer team come into play. The hardest thing I ever had to do was sit down with adoption paperwork and fill out an absolutely hideous, truth-requiring, heart-wrenching document. Could I handle a child that was HIV positive, drug-dependent, or had been sexually abused?

When I first saw that paperwork, I was frightened, overwhelmed, and livid. Every description I read broke my heart. These groups of children, which possibly included my own soon-to-be child, had been abused by the world and attacked by Satan in the most evil of ways. In my mommy heart, I wanted to rescue every child and begin the work of loving those kiddos. In order to move forward, I had to really face the truth and lay it all out before God—could I handle a child with a difficult past? Was I ready to accept certain special needs? Was I equipped and supported to be the mommy this child would need?

If you are called to parent a child who has lived through trauma or who has special needs, God will grant you an extra measure (or many measures) of grace. At that moment of truth, I had to honestly say where I was spiritually, parentally, and practically while taking my existing family into consideration. And it was so hard. I cried over this, and I prayed it up and down.

The social worker had advised me to fill this form out separately from the Hubs and then for us to come together to talk and pray. This was invaluable advice for us, for it allowed us both to be honest and to discern what God was leading us to do. Know that God isn't about division in family. He will not tell you something different from your spouse! The hard moment eased for us after we knew we had handled this difficult portion of the journey together with Jesus.

If you feel you need to review this form together, go for it! The separate approach worked for us because I needed silence to really hear God speak, but do what's right for you. Looking back now, there were many benefits to this exercise, but there were two I kept coming back to over and over. First, I was not called to parent every child. I was not placed here to rescue the world; I was called to find my child. In my mind, the exact child that our Most High God created was waiting for me, and I was going to fight like crazy to bring him or her home. Second, I needed to know my limits, and once I knew them, I needed to be willing to let God work. You see, one of the things I was privately afraid of in my own heart was parenting a child with special needs.

Special needs is a very large gray area in adoption paperwork. It can mean anything from multiethnic or multi-birth to profound neurological disorders. Please understand that an orphanage in Uganda or Asia could have very different parameters in describing special needs than would an American pediatrician. Of course, this is where prayer comes in, friends!

As the emotional mommy that I am, I sobbed over this document, meaning that I ugly cried. Then I had to release it for us to move forward. God took that document, took my crying heart, and said, "I see you claim these limits right now. I see you praying over every one of these hundreds of pages of paperwork, and I've chosen your child for your family before the foundation of the world." After all that emotional energy was spent, it was back to "hurry up and wait" mode. After many months, we saw our baby boy. He was beautiful, (oh my—so beautiful!) and he was home!

When he was six months old, like any overexcited mommy, I dressed him up like pint-sized royalty and took him out for the traditional six-month pediatric visit. I was fully expecting and even craving the "oohs" and "aahs" I was now accustomed to during each of our well-child visits. This was no sick check; we were there to be paraded around and loved on. But this time we weren't meeting developmental standards. His weight was low, and his physical feats were not on par with his age. Thus began a several-months-long journey of research, phone calls, and trying to figure out what in the world was going on. There were blood tests at the largest children's hospital in our state, neurological tests with our chiropractor, and documentation upon documentation of anecdotal notes on his daily routine, eating preferences, and sleeping habits. I honestly was fairly obnoxious in pushing through obstacles, and God bless it, that's what my baby boy deserved, for that's what all kids deserve. We finally gained entry into the most precious of early intervention organizations: Babies Can't Wait.

When he was 10 months old, we suddenly had a new support team consisting of our pediatrician, neurological chiropractor, physical therapist, speech pathologist, and a supervisor. The fear I once had of parenting a special needs child had come to fruition despite the fact that our son had the most in-depth medical history of any member of my family, whether biological or adopted.

All the information you get from your social worker or agency is good and important, but it is not the be-all and end-all. At times, an adoptive parent might be prone to think how easy biological families have it because they know so much or can do so much prenatally for their children. But I know sweet, prayerful biological parents who have been blown away by special needs diagnoses or other medical diagnoses that they were not expecting.

It comes down to knowing yourself and knowing your God. Be honest, but be open! God's providential will prevails whether we want to play ball or not, whether we are comfortable or not, and whether we feel prepared or not. Hold tight to this truth: His will is good, both for you and your child. Will you allow yourself to be used, to be a willing participant in His plan, even if it varies wildly from your own? This is important to consider.

Looking back now, I feel so humbled. God has given me the ability to be a stay-at-home mom for almost 10 years now. I have worked in different capacities from home, at one point even nannying and bringing the baby with me. I realize now that my specific children needed the daily, possibly overbearing, in-your-face mommying that I was desperate to give after years of waiting. I had over 10 years of experience in education from early childhood education on up. I had professional experience teaching in inclusion classrooms, and I had been privileged to work closely with a variety of special needs educators. God had even given me professional experience implementing special needs therapy for kids in my old classrooms. All this life experience was not an accident. It was divine preparation.

I had to fight for months on end to have others recognize my son's delays as actual delays and not just his personality. Without consciously realizing it, I had learned from the parents who fought tooth and nail for their children on the other side of my desk. I found a community who "got it," and marched forward into a parenting season I had never considered. Oh my gracious, y'all, I am so grateful for this season. Is it hard? Yes! Do I feel seriously ill-equipped at times? I do. Would I change it for anything? No, I would not change this for the world.

In short, I am so not a perfect mother. But I am the perfect mommy for my littles. And you will be for your child, too! You are specifically gifted for exactly what he or she needs, and your child is a gift to you. This does not mean you are a perfect person, but that it is God's will, and therefore part of His perfect plan, for you to be the parent of your child. This totally reminds me of a sign I used to have in my elementary classroom, which stated, "All kids are gifted...some just open their gifts at a different time than others." My son isn't Special Needs; he *has* some special needs. Because I was so attuned to him as a person, I saw things early that others might have missed. I had the knowledge and background that prepared me for the initial battle. God will prepare you, too!

God knew better than me, and I am in tears thinking of all we would have missed if God let me wallow in my "I can't," instead of letting Him help me realize that He always can! So please remember that although information is good, surprises can still come. Don't get lost in the ideals you create and miss out on God's ideal idea. His ideas are always better!

Daddy's Take:

I remember very little of the paperwork we had to fill out because it included massive amounts of information. However, that one piece of paper remains unforgettable. Considering special needs was kind of scary for both of us. We wanted to make sure we were honest and really considered what we could handle. The funny thing is that God can handle anything. And He has. He has brought in the experts, professionals, respite, and encouragers as we've needed them. We have learned so much about ourselves and the tenderness of God toward His children. It was a surprise, but neither of us would ever change it.

Scripture for Your Journey:

Proverbs 3:6
In all your ways submit to him,
and he will make your paths straight.

Jeremiah 29:11
For I know the plans I have for you, declares the Lord, plans for welfare and not for evil, to give you a future and a hope.

Prayer for Your Journey:

Dear Jesus,
Thank You for information—it is good, and it is needed. We are walking a journey where we get very little of it at times, so we are grateful for what we

do receive. But Lord, please don't let us stay stuck in analysis paralysis, trying to figure out the best way through the information overload. Please don't let us create fears in our own mind about what may be. Let us acknowledge the information, release our concerns, and walk confidently in the knowledge that You have led us to this place because You have a very specific child that You handpicked for our family. And You handpicked us for them. Thank You, Lord, for being sovereign and good all of the time. In Your name we pray. Amen.

Action Points:

1. How will you deal with information overload?
2. With whom will you share these decision points?
3. How will you decide what you can handle? Here are some tools: fasting, prayer, and seeking out your adoption team's input.
4. How much of the more challenging information do you feel led to share with others? Why? Do you feel led to share because you want accountability and prayer or because you feel like you have to?

NOTES

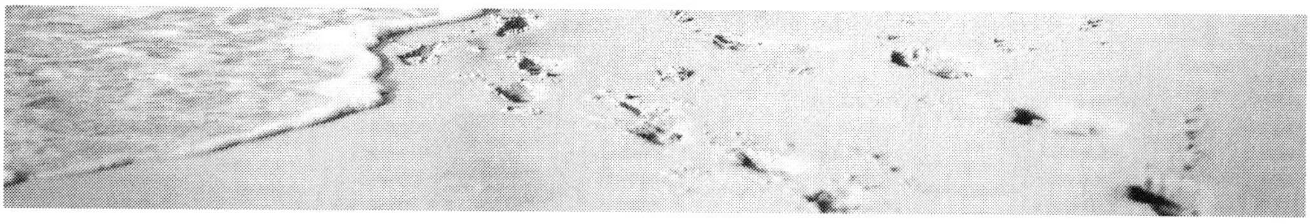

NOTES

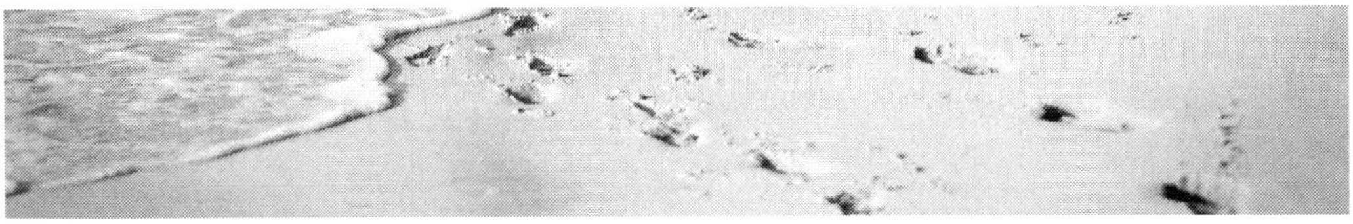

Chapter 15

TRAUMA AND TRIUMPH

When we dream about a future adoptive placement, our hearts go warm and fuzzy, our view may suddenly appear rose-colored. If you are like me, it's possible that the pragmatic part of you might start considering school options, furniture placement, or how you'll introduce your new addition to the rest of your family.

What I've realized about myself is that I am *Optimistic* with a capital "O." My strongest spiritual gift is faith. Combine these two things and I can be awesome at praying down mountains and banging on the gates of heaven. The flip side is that I feel side-swiped when things do not work out the way I expected. I'm surprised when my circumstances don't happen exactly how I planned—I mean prayed.

I've had to accept and lean into the truth that God is never surprised by the happy or by the hard. With time and the wisdom of some great mommy-mentors, I've learned that my *Good Plans* may not always be (almost always are not) *God's Plans*. The other thing I have to be at peace with, even when it's hard to embrace, is that everything we experience here on earth is sifted through God's hand.

This is especially important to remember when we think about Big, Hairy, Awful Circumstances (BHAC?), for instance, a kid who has experienced hard things. Especially when that kid could be YOUR KID. In my Mama Bear heart, I begin to roar, "God, where were you? God, how could you? God, it is too much, too big, too hard!" Each time I go there—into my fear—I start to feel the Spirit resonate with the words: "Peace. Be still" (Mark 4:39, NKJV).

A big huge reframe is in order, and it is needed quickly. I have to use my coping tools and breathe through it, count my blessings, and sometimes even snap a hairband on my wrist to regroup. No, Jacqui, God did not "Do this" to anyone. Yes, Jacqui, God is still in control and weeps when His children are hurting. Yes, Jacqui, He is still the God of miracles and works in the details of our lives . . . if we let Him. As I tell our kids all the time, Jesus is a gentleman and will not push His way into our everyday affairs. We need to invite Him to come in.

This is the hard part . . . and I share with you not to scare you, but to prepare you. Adoption for you may be a calling, an answered prayer, or a way to finally experience your dream of a family. I get this. It has been that for me too. But for a child who is in foster care, an orphanage, a group home, or who is having an adoption plan made, your answered prayer may feel like his or her biggest nightmare. So this is when we put on our big girl (boy) pants and remember that FEELINGS ARE NOT FACTS!

The thing I had to learn, and that I sometimes (often) need to be reminded about, is that God is in control. Stated another way—I am NOT in control. And y'all, that's a good thing. My fixes are short-sighted and really focused on pushing the uncomfortable unknown away, rather than attempting to focus on the eternal. I'm getting better about reining in my "feelings" and letting God be God. But it has taken many years and much hard work. Basically, I had to learn that God is a way better god than I could ever be.

The second thing I had to get real about is that I can't see the whole picture. I don't fully understand the immediate, the eternal, or the symbiotic relationship between the spiritual and natural. When God allows hard things to happen, especially to children, or especially to MY children, I rail, and cry, and gnash my teeth. But when I step back, I begin to see.

If Romans 8:28 applies to me, then it also applies to my kids. So all things work together for good for all of us. When you pull back the scriptures and take the word "all" down to its Latin roots, "all" means . . . ALL! If you are like me, this is the moment when I regroup and recognize that I am NOT the Lord, and that is a good thing. His ways are higher than our ways. (Isaiah 55:8) And God is good and overflows with loving kindness and faithfulness. (Psalm 100:5)

I believe that when bad, evil things happen to His people, Jesus weeps with us. I believe this is a broken world and, because of the Fall in the Garden of Eden, we experience things we were never meant to experience: things that feel too big, too bad, and too much. I believe deep in my Momma Heart that He wired me to care about justice and protecting kids.

The Bible says, "But whoever causes one of these little ones who believe in me to sin, it would be **better** for him to have a great **millstone** fastened **around** his **neck** and to be drowned in the depth of the sea" (Matthew 18:6). Knowing the character of God, I believe that anyone who hurts one of these little ones will experience the wrath of God. However, my flesh and my spirit have to accept that I may not see that justice. I may have to walk through the hard parts of healing and helping a child who is carrying more than any person was ever meant to carry and trust God to carry out His justice.

For some of you, that may mean loving and parenting a child who has had a drug exposure in utero. For others, that may be helping a child reconcile their birth story and backstory with the goodness of God the Father.

For a few parents, there may even be a spiritual battle for a child's innocence and purity because of someone else's evil sin. Wherever you are, whatever you are facing, God isn't surprised. He is more than equal to the crisis even when, or especially when, we just aren't.

There is power in prayer. Pray that child, your family, their therapy team, and teachers up and down. And as this kid's main caregiver, as their Momma and Papa Bear, pray yourselves up and down too. You need the prayer coverage to dig into the resiliency and the faith that will see y'all through. You will need your tribe around you to offer respite, rest, encouragement, and hope for the hardest times. You will need to pray for ears to hear, because the enemy cannot wait to scream his favorite lies:

- You can't handle this. (You can't, but God can!)
- You made a mistake. (God already gave us James 1:27—no mistake—you are in His will.)
- You have hurt the rest of your family by walking into this space. (Right there I say a holy *No* to the lies of the enemy!)

Jesus is in the business of miracles, healing, and igniting hope! Jesus is the author of life, family, and faith. You are called into this, and He was not just testing your obedience. This is your kiddo—this is your story of faith and family. Yes, it may feel messy and ugly at times, but God is in the business of giving beauty for ashes and turning trauma into triumph. Lean into Him and watch the healing—for all of you—begin!

(For additional information on trauma please consider reading *The Body Keeps the Score* by Bessel Van Der Kolk or the *Summary of The Body Keeps the Score.*)

Daddy's Take:

- Over half of all children in the world—1 billion children ages 2–17 years—experience violence every year. This and more data can be found on the CDC website (cdc.gov/violenceprevention/childabuseandneglect).
- Complex ongoing trauma impacts the body, brain and beliefs.
- If you feel ill-equipped, get down on your knees first. Then use the internet for good and start to learn about trauma, attachment, and healing. Start to use what you know with your family. Ask God to bless it and reveal your next steps. Ask Him to move and watch what He does.

Scripture for Your Journey:

Mark 4:39, NKJV
Peace. Be still.

Isaiah 55:8
"For my thoughts are not your thoughts, neither are your ways my ways," declares the Lord.

Psalm 100:5
For the Lord is good and his love endures forever; his faithfulness continues through all generations.

Matthew 18:6
"If anyone causes one of these little ones—those who believe in me—to stumble, it would be better for them to have a large millstone hung around their neck and to be drowned in the depths of the sea."

James 1:27
Religion that God our Father accepts as pure and faultless is this: to look after orphans and widows in their distress and to keep oneself from being polluted by the world.

Prayer for Your Journey:

Jesus,
Sometimes our children experience the face of evil. They endure hardships we have never considered and don't even know how to pray against. We feel hurt that our children have been hurt, and we feel ill equipped to help them heal. The world would say we were crazy to try. The enemy will tell us it is a pointless journey, to get out while we still can. But Jesus, we lean into You. We ask you for Your holy will over our child, our family, and our own hearts. We ask you to take this from test to testimony. Send every resource, encouragement, and provision we need to help our child grow into the person You have designed him or her to be. Help us to find joy in the midst of sorrow. Redeem what the enemy wanted to steal. We give You praise for the victory. In Jesus' name, we pray. Amen and Amen.

Action Points:

1. Be very intentional and wise about what you share with others regarding your child's history, exposure, etc. But be bold in advocating for your child with health caregivers, therapists, counselors, etc. (Personal aside: before every IEP meeting, intervention, or new program, pray with all those involved in the care and healing of your child. Include all who will be an influence over your child's welfare, regardless of where they are in their faith journey. It will be a testimony for the watching world and will bring the Holy Spirit into the space immediately.)
2. Remember your self-care. (I know!) You need to be healthy to help them heal. Be mindful of time with safe friends with whom you can share the joys and the messy. Get outside in nature to walk, run, and experience God's glorious goodness. Journal, eat well, and SLEEP. It's more than just okay to take care of you. It is necessary!
3. Allow others to minister to you. Even though it may be easier for you to be the caregiver instead of the care receiver, if your people want to help with childcare, meals, laundry, etc., say YES! You will have a chance to pay it forward later, but right now, let the body of Christ be the hands and feet of Jesus to you and yours.

NOTES

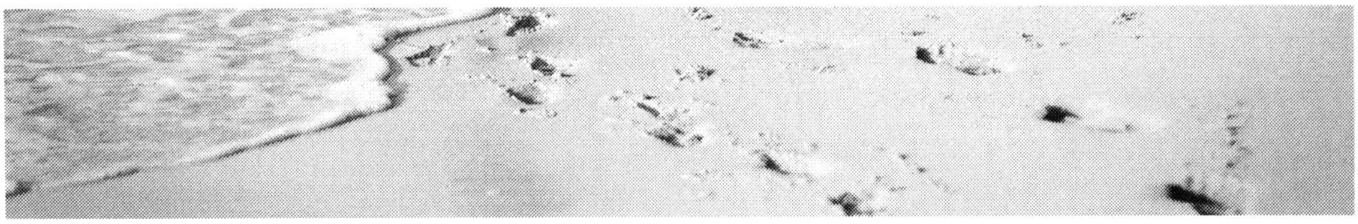

NOTES

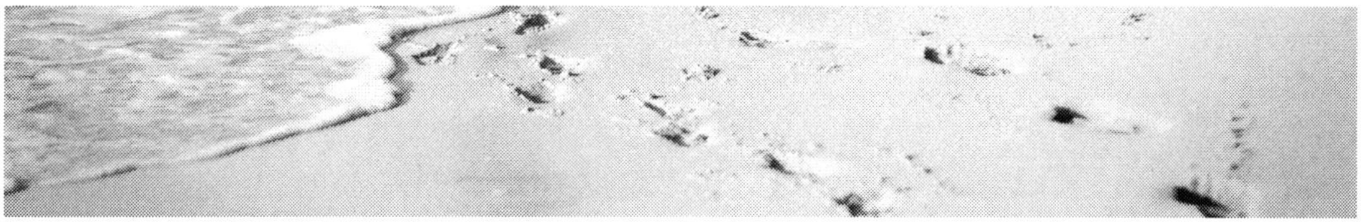

Chapter 16

PRAYING WISDOM THROUGH THE WANT

If you are like the many prospective parents I know, you really, really want your child to be here. You are probably fantasizing about what the next addition to your family will look like, be like, and become one day. On good days, I could picture myself playing outside in the backyard as the sun began to set and the humidity lessened. I could see a little brown-haired girl running to me. I could feel my heart swell as she was about to jump into my arms. I was in love. I was in desperate want, and I don't believe I handled this precious time of preparation in the best of ways during that particular season. I had moments of clarity, direction, and prayerful rest, but I also had a lot of moments stuck in my flesh, wandering and wondering. I'll share the highlights of both ends of the spectrum.

The Good:

The interim months between the home study and the call were filled with less intentionality during my first adoption process, but my second was different. During my daughter's adoption process, I spent an inordinate amount of time fretting: each time the phone rang, I about fell out as I raced to answer it. I was prepared for months on end for the voice on the other line to announce the longed-for information giving details about my future child. For some reason, I never checked the caller ID, convinced as I was that the call was imminent. It wasn't long off, but it surely took longer than my hopeful heart was prepared for. To be completely honest, I thought that at the conclusion of our home visit, our sweet adoption worker would pull out a sonogram right then and there as a surprise. That was not the case!

I spent the intervening months attending monthly parenting classes with the adoption agency and filling journal upon journal with my thoughts, dreams, and fears. I began a phone call campaign with intensity, taking it upon myself to call said unsuspecting social worker weekly to remind her, "Yep, we still want a baby!" In all honesty, I would still do that. But equally as important, I now realize, are the areas of personal growth that I did not embrace during the first adoption.

I did not use this time to really grow in my faith, so God grew me with the wait and the want through wisdom. The hardest lesson to learn was that I had to want Jesus more than I wanted my precious child. This lesson was not easy, and I fought it for a long time. But in His goodness and grace, He gave me the opportunity for a do-over with my second child, and it went a little differently.

Whereas ignorance was bliss with the first, I was "older and wiser" to this whole adoption game in the second round. From the get-go, I still had some of the same issues to deal with, along with some new ones to add to it! Gracious. Through experience, though, I knew how to handle these struggles better.

One of the best things I did with the second child was to prepare my daughter's heart for this transition. Together we read Scripture, prayed for our baby (not mommy's baby—we were all waiting for *our* baby), decorated the nursery, picked out baby items, and even trained for and ran a race in support of adoption.

In an effort to fundraise for the second adoption, I began to train with a friend for a half-marathon at Disney World, as I described in a previous chapter—and of which I'm apparently quite proud! Running had become my go-to for stress management years before, and raising awareness about adoption, and, more specifically, raising funds for our family's adoption, really resonated with me. By then, I was no longer working full-time, so I wanted to offset the cost of this second adventure. Plus, I wanted to do *something*! Sitting quietly and waiting has never been my style, so this was a perfect fit.

Training began in earnest and culminated in a weekend trip to see Mickey Mouse himself. My daughter's race was on Saturday (and she rocked it with her three-year-old self!), and my half marathon began Sunday morning at 5:30 am. I wore a T-shirt highlighting our adoption to let the world know that I was running in honor of our baby. Disney surprised us with buttons that said, "Ask me about our adoption," and there was even a "Big Sister" button for my daughter. I had the opportunity to share about our calling with many people, and during that race, God spoke in a mighty way to my heart.

The Bad:

The big-sibling preparation and the fundraising were both awesome ideas. However, on a personal level, God was still working on patience and peace in my heart.

After the excitement of the race, we had about four to five months of silence. Our paperwork was submitted, but we were in a stalemate with the home study process. I still desperately wanted and did not enjoy the wait!

It was hard to watch other families lap us—with two, three, and even five children, while we were still waiting to find our second. It was hard to hear people say casually how they were expecting biologically "by accident." It was confusing—did we not hear God? Did we answer someone else's calling? I began to "what if" myself, which my small group of girlfriends from ages ago will shout to the rafters means "what I fear!" And that was it: I feared that I would never be a mother to multiple children. What I feared was releasing that dream.

The Ugly:

One day, God leveled me. He held me, called me His daughter, and gently, in peace and patience, asked if I would love Him if I never had more children. Would I praise Him if this storm had no end? I wrestled, I fought, and finally, I surrendered. I thought, "Yes, Lord, I will love You, no matter what. I will praise You even if You say no. But precious Jesus, take this desire away from me. Please don't leave me here in this broken, confused, sad little state. If my calling is my husband and the daughter sleeping down the hall, then please, please remove all other desires right now, today."

I remember this moment, for we had been in this particular process for one year. For any of you who have had this want in your heart for a matter of time, the one-year, two-year, or more mark is slightly devastating. Paperwork has to be re-upped. More fees may be assessed. And another calendar page is torn away.

This "Come to Jesus" meeting happened as I ran through the historical town square near our home. I was listening to Steve Fee on an iPod, and praying really hard when God spoke. As I listened at that moment, I felt two things: A total weight was removed from my head and shoulders, and then I felt a peace that surpasses understanding. I began to cry. At first, it was one little, glistening tear that probably caught the sunlight and looked very sedate. Quickly, because it's me, and I'm classy, it turned to ugly crying, and I ran through the now-busy, shopper-infested historic district attempting to find my car through a haze of tears. It wasn't sadness, or frustration, or angst that propelled this intense wave of emotion; it was a knowing deep in my spirit that somewhere in the heavenlies, God was moving on our behalf.

At that exact second, I thought perhaps that was the feeling of release and that God was removing the desire from my heart to replace it with His desire and my contentment in the season I was in. I had asked God to do it, and this immediate emotional reaction seemed to confirm that yes, I was a mommy to one precious daughter and the wife to one precious man and that was God's dream for me—but no!

I finally found my car and started mopping my tears before immediately calling my younger and wiser sister to share what had happened. She counseled me to immediately journal the feelings, the time, and the date. She mentioned that she thought it had to do with my baby, that something may have been happening right then, and I needed to pray hard. I prayed and wrote, and let me tell you this: The day this happened, the birth mother of our sweet child, who knew us not, and of whom we had no knowledge, went into labor. As I prayed and released and recognized that no matter what, I wanted Jesus even more than I wanted a child, God moved. He moved mountains. He moved in me, and He moved for me.

Daddy's Take:

The wait is just hard. For me, I could stay busy with the family right in front of me and the work God had given me. For my wife, it was way different. She had left her career to focus on our family—she handled the bulk of the paperwork, the phone calls, and the fundraising. Because this process essentially became her job, it really overwhelmed her. The way God grew me was to mold me into the prayerful husband I always wanted to be, knew

I needed to be, but now had to be. I prayed over the child we parented daily, and I prayed over the child we'd never even held as well. I prayed for my own growth, and I prayed for peace for my wife's heart. Today, I am so grateful for the growth we all experienced, including the growing pains that come with expanding a family, for we experienced it God's way.

Scripture for Your Journey:

Luke 14:25–26
Large crowds were traveling with Jesus, and turning to them he said: "If anyone comes to me and does not hate father and mother, wife and children, brothers and sisters—yes, even their own life—such a person cannot be my disciple."
(Commentary note: Read hate as a comparative. Compared to your heart for and surrender to Jesus, anything else would look like hate. It's not saying that you actually hate your family members.)

Job 12:13
To God belong wisdom and power;
counsel and understanding are his.

Prayer for Your Journey:

Dear Jesus,
Please hold us close during our wait. It may be a quick journey, or it may take quite a while. Be gentle with us. Connect us deeply to You, deeply into a community that supports us, and deeply to the child for whom we long. Even as we wait to find out where this child is and when we will all meet, let our hearts stay closely connected to You. We praise You for your kindness in dealing with our tired hearts. Amen.

Action Points:

1. What are your deepest wants or worries? How can you release these to Jesus and let Him bear the burden?

2. How are you using the interim time? Should you begin using it differently?
3. What is an area that you can work on now that will prepare you for the joys of parenting your newest addition later? This could include parenting class, adoption connections, and/or cultural studies if your adoption journey is international or transracial.

NOTES

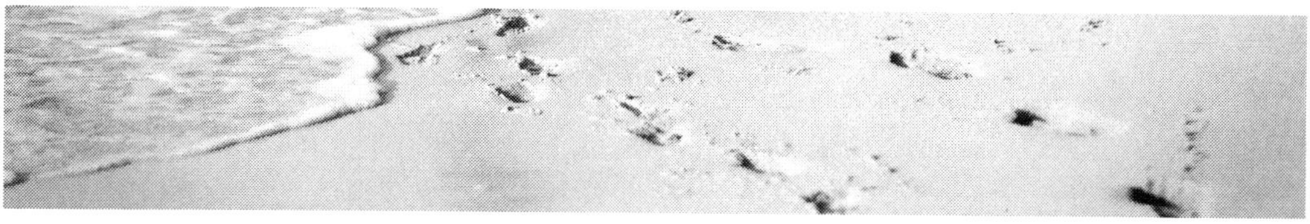

NOTES

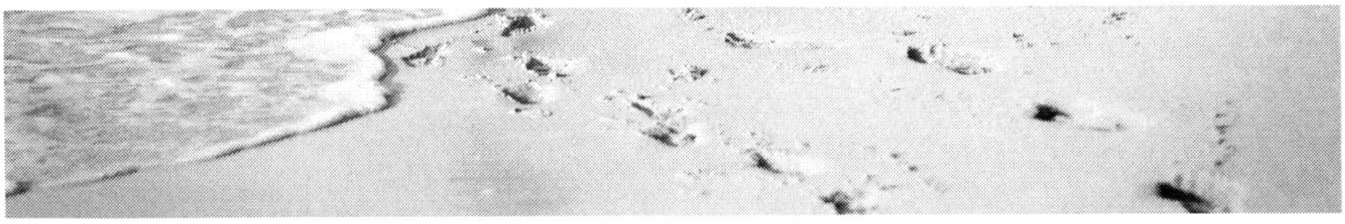

Chapter 17

WHEN THINGS GO SIDEWAYS, TRY, TRY AGAIN

The difficulties may be greater for some than for others who are called to adopt. That is simply a fact, albeit a frustrating one that I have a hard time accepting. Just as in a biological addition, some couples glide through with nary a complication, while others face loss, infertility, and other hardships. No matter how God calls you to build your family, there is the possibility of heartache, but take heart: The end result when you hold your child for the first time is completely worth anything you have to go through to find him or her. I firmly believe that and have experienced it personally.

I want to be very intentional not to perpetuate what I term the "Lifetime Movie of the Week" drama, for this process has enough dramatic twists and turns to fill several TV seasons on its own. Everyone has heard of that person or couple who has been traumatized by a "failed adoption"—a legalish term that my heart opposes greatly. Does it happen? Yes, it does, but for all the terror this term connotes and all the anxiety it engenders in a waiting heart, it is not as common as we fear. But dear reader, it is so very hard to pray through a journey, put yourself out there in faith, and hit what seems like one closed door after another. Even more disheartening is the thought that you could walk right into the "winner's circle" of matching, meeting, and more, and still have the wheels come off this thing. That is why I pray that you walk firmly in faith. The only thing that got me through the times that felt like everything was falling to absolute pieces was my faith, which admittedly felt shaky during those moments.

A while back, I found out through family friends that a sweet baby was born in my old college town on a night I was in town for a college football game. I nicknamed him NoMo because I have chosen a prayer name from the Bible for every child I have been blessed to pray for, long for, and finally welcome into this family. Mo stood for Moses, the first example of infant adoption found in Scripture. NoMo was a precious baby boy, and he was found in swaddling clothes, literally, in the downtown area in the wee hours of the morning. My heart fell in love, sight unseen, and I went to work hounding the agency. It seemed obvious to me that I was supposed to adopt him because I was right there when he was born. The wait for my ongoing adoption journey was clocking in at almost one year, and I was ready to be a momma.

I spent 24 hours demon-dialing the agency with calls and voicemails while longing for the child. Finally, I learned that NoMo was under the protection of state custody and not eligible for an interstate adoption. Ugly crying ensued. Although this experience was a long way from the severity of hardships other families have faced, it was deeply upsetting.

That wasn't my Mo, but even to this day, I still find myself remembering that child, thinking about that child, and yes, even praying for that specific child. So perhaps my small role in hearing of his dramatic entrance into this world is to pray him home. I honestly believe one day we will meet in heaven. Although my heart hurt at the time because I was denied what I longed for, his soul was not the one I was meant to parent.

I found out exactly one month later that my forever daughter would be due in three weeks. Within a seven-week period, I went from longing, begging, and feeling confused to busy maternity preparations. As a total aside, for those of you adopting for the first time, be prepared for intense pregnancy-like symptoms to ensue once you have your own "due date"—insomnia, nausea, and tearful emotional reactions can all be experienced at a full tilt! Is it exhausting? Yes. Is it worth it? Absolutely!

I also have had prayerful, faithful cousins walk a four-year journey to find their sweet daughter. Their story is covered with the fingerprints of God, and I believe He orchestrated their story to reach many for His kingdom.

The hardest part was watching my sweet, dear friend walk through the wait while praying alongside her and knowing in-depth the brokenness she felt as it seemed as if life just fell apart. But God is so good, y'all. He is faithful. What the enemy intended for destruction, God used for good, and their daughter is home! I simply couldn't do justice to their story, so grab some tissues, and jump into this incredible God-moment that is shared in Jillian's own words:

"Our adoption story began four years ago. We had always wanted to adopt, and the timing just seemed right since it was time to give our daughter a little brother or sister. We started looking into both domestic and international options, but all the doors were closing other than foster care through our local county. We signed up to take foster care classes and became licensed foster/adoptive parents through the Department of Social Services. On November 4, 2012, we received a call that there was a one-day-old little boy who needed a safe place to go. We were told that there was a 99% chance this precious baby would become available for adoption. We quickly said yes and over the course of the next ten months loved, cared, and prayed over our sweet Elijah. During this time, God burdened our hearts for his birth parents, and we prayed every morning at our kitchen table that his parents would come to know the Lord and that the patterns of addiction would be broken through the power of Jesus.

"Over time, we built a trusting relationship with them and encouraged them any chance we got. In the fall of 2013, Elijah's birth mother came to a large church event with us, gave her life to the Lord, and was baptized. Plans changed after that, and we sent our foster son back home to his parents in September of 2013. Our hearts were so thrilled for them to have their son back home, yet so broken for us—we loved Elijah as our own and missed him terribly. How would our daughter ever recover from losing the only sibling she had ever had? We constantly reminded her of God's goodness despite our circumstances, and that He would be faithful to complete what He had called us to do.

"Much to our delight, Elijah's parents asked us on the day he returned to them to become his godparents and to still be active and involved in his life. To this day, two and a half years later, we still see Elijah often. He comes to stay with our family every other weekend, and we love him more now as our "son" than we ever dreamed possible.

"After Elijah left, our hearts still longed for a child whom we could bring into our family through adoption. Our sole purpose in adopting, after all, was to give a child who would never have the opportunity to know and learn about Christ the opportunity to know Him. We knew God was specifically calling us to grow our family through adoption. We knew we couldn't go through foster care again because it had devastated our daughter when Elijah left. We had to find an option where we could bring a child home who would never have to leave. And so our journey to adopt through domestic private adoption began.

"In July of 2014, we were matched with a beautiful birth mother in Florida, who was giving birth to a baby boy in December. She had made an adoption plan and selected us as his parents. Our amazing friends and family helped us fundraise every penny that it took to adopt domestically, and we were simply blown away at God's provision. It was beyond clear that His will was for us to adopt this little boy. His name would be Josiah Elijah. His first name was after King Josiah of the Bible, one of the greatest kings to ever rule. King Josiah followed God all the days of his life, and we couldn't think of a more appropriate name. His middle name would be after our foster son, now godson, who had a very special place in our hearts.

"Over days and weeks, we grew to love and care deeply for the birth mother and again prayed each morning at our kitchen table that she would come to know Jesus. We were blessed to have the opportunity to travel to meet her in October of 2014 and to spend a weekend getting to know her. It was much to our surprise that we received a heart-rending phone call from her on December 1, 2014, just two days before we were to travel to Florida to bring our son home. During that call, she informed me that she had already given birth to Josiah on Thanksgiving Day and that her plan had changed from adoption to parenting.

"Our hearts were completely shattered, and the grief was almost unbearable. We had to tell our daughter once again that she was not going to have a baby brother, but to believe that God was still faithful. It was the most awful day of my life. I truly had no idea that a seven-year-old could even grieve like that.

"Just four days later, on December 5, 2014, I went to Elijah's house to pick him up for the weekend. We thought it would be best to get our minds off things and to let our daughter have a fun few days with her God-brother. Upon arriving at his house for pickup, I told his mother the story of how our adoption had failed. She immediately began telling me of a friend of hers who was looking for adoptive parents! Her friend was scheduled to meet with an adoption agency the next day, so she told me to call her friend right away if we were interested. We, of course, were beyond interested but were careful to guard our hearts because of the grief we were still experiencing over Josiah.

"The following day, a friend of mine went with me to her house and we all quickly realized that this was a perfect match. The baby's birth mother ended up telling the adoption agency she was no longer interested in their services because she had found the adoptive parents she was looking for. From that point on, I began taking her back and forth to baby checkup appointments and grew a relationship with her over a period of two and a half months. I was even blessed to be at the hospital for our daughter's delivery and witnessed her being brought into the world.

"Our second daughter was born on February 20, 2015. She is healthy, strong, and incredibly beautiful. We surprised our first daughter with a new baby sister whom she had no idea was coming! She was very excited to finally be a big sister and told me the day she met her little sister that being a big sister was everything she had ever dreamed of. My heart is so full sometimes that it literally feels like it may burst out of my chest.

"The most overwhelming part of our adoption story for me is that the relationship we worked so hard to create with our foster son's mother directly influenced us adopting our second daughter. I could never in a million years have imagined that she would be the one to help us find our daughter.

"Our adoption story is filled with more twists and turns than I ever wanted, but it was worth every heartache and tear now that we have our daughter home. I will never be able to tell the Lord enough times how good He is. I will never in all my days be able to sing Him the praises He is so worthy of. I will never understand why He chose us to impact these little souls. But there is one thing I do know and understand: Sweet Baby Girl, *you are chosen*. You are adopted. You are loved. And above all, God, You are faithful!"

Oh my! The takeaway? God keeps His promises. His covenant promises that we find in the Word and that He whispers to our hearts do not fail. My experience with NoMo was so limited comparatively, but it confused me, scared me, and sadly made me doubt if I was on the right path. My cousin's story is probably one of those which, if told in part rather than in its entirety, could really scare prospective parents into that analysis paralysis we spoke of earlier. Hard times happened, but as this family shares, God used everything. God held them together. God brought their daughter home!

In the midst of devastating heartbreak, He was still working. God remained on the throne watching it all. The wheels in heaven kept turning, and my cousins now have the honor and privilege of stewarding two sweet little souls to heaven.

No matter what you hear, what you experience, and what heartaches you have endured thus far, your calling and effort to bring it to fruition is not in vain. With adoption it really isn't if; it's when. Claim that now, and know I am praying alongside you. Godspeed!

Daddy's Take:

I remember praying daily with our family for our cousins' adoption. I can still remember what my heart felt like when we found out that the plan we had all thought was coming together suddenly changed. It brought back a lot of the feelings Jacqui and I had experienced in our season of waiting. It reminded us both about how critical it is to pray God's best. His will is Good, and His timing is perfect, but sometimes in our humanity, it feels so hard. Stay connected to your team, to your spouse, and to the God who's really got this! He truly does.

Scripture for Your Journey:

Proverbs 4:23
Above all else, guard your heart,
for everything you do flows from it.

Romans 8:28–29
[2]*And we know that in all things God works for the good of those who love him, who have been called according to his purpose.* [29] *For those God foreknew he also predestined to be conformed to the image of his Son, that he might be the firstborn among many brothers and sisters.*

Prayer for Your Journey:

Dear Jesus,
As we step out in faith for our child-to-be, we know that we can't see the whole path. You light only the step right in front of us at times, and sometimes that next step feels so very scary. It may not feel like we thought it would, it may not be as easy as we wanted it to be, and it may ask more of us than we thought we could give, but Jesus, You are a Good, Good, Father. You are bringing us into a miracle. You have a good plan for each of us. Hold us Father, especially when the hard gets harder. Hold us when we feel we may break. And Jesus, please be gentle with us. Please take us from test to testimony for your glory and for our good. Amen.

Action Points:

1. If you have faced this kind of loss or heartbreak, please take the time you need to heal, pray, and regroup. This time is essential to be open, communicative, and to grieve. It is real, and it is hard.
2. Where do you go from here? Ask for and accept Godly counsel. Perhaps you are called to press on just as you have been. Some families have recognized that God used the so-called setback to move them to a new path that led to their child.
3. Do you have fears about those "Lifetime Movie" situations? Discuss them honestly, and release them.
4. If you feel that the unwashed masses are giving you more discouragement, pray that God will give you an equal or bolder measure of encouragement. Pray and actively look for families who have successfully adopted no matter what obstacle befell them, and rest in those victories!

NOTES

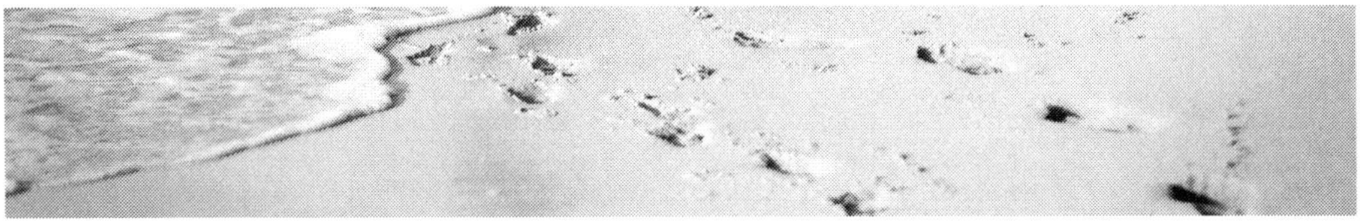

NOTES

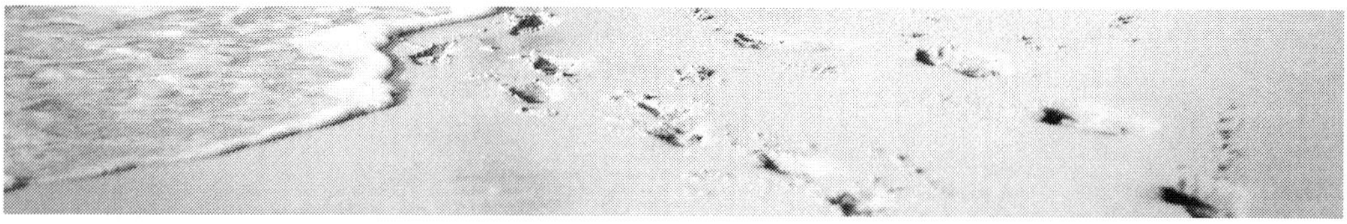

Chapter 18

A PICTURE IS WORTH 1,000 WORDS AND 10,000 EMOTIONS

Well, this is a big time. After much prayer and reflection, many hundreds of pages of paperwork, and the interminable wait, you have probably received the greatly coveted picture. For some, it comes in an email attachment. For others, it is an actual photograph. For me, it was an ultrasound image.

However and whenever you receive it, it will rock your world in the most majestic of ways because now you know! Please know that if you have not yet received an image, you need not fret! I pray that it comes soon, but if not, know that God has still got this. Even if your first glimpse of your child is in person, that's perfectly okay!

After weeks, months, or possibly years of being paper pregnant, you now know who your child is and where your child is. More importantly, you likely have more than an inkling of when you will get to squeeze that sweet little one and kiss those cheeks.

I remember when I first got my daughter's picture. After a long day teaching junior high school students, I had finally completed the week's grading, so I showered and prepared to journal to my then unborn, unmet baby-to-be. Having received "the call" only eight days prior, I had begun to walk to my own drumbeat, or at least to my relentless heartbeat as it reverberated soundlessly through my body saying, "You're a mommy, you're a mommy, you're a mommy." Since "the call," that refrain pounded endlessly and powerfully, and it became a much-welcomed background track to my life. I padded out in slippers and yoga pants to check the mail, prepared for a quiet evening. In the midst of bills and junk mail was a legal-sized envelope from the adoption agency. I brought it inside, opened it up, and hit my knees.

I was holding a photograph that changed my life. A simple ultrasound photo of my much beloved, long-awaited daughter fell into my hands, and I just started sobbing. I clutched that sweet gift to my chest and shared that first mommy moment with Jesus.

I could see her little hand up next to her cheeks. I could see her sweet mouth. She was perfect and beautiful in every way; she had been perfectly formed in her birth-mother's womb. Glancing at the floor, I noticed a sticky note had fallen out. It was a note from the social worker saying that my baby's birth mother had asked her to send this to me. She wanted me to have it because she thought I would like to see what my daughter looked like at this moment in her development. That remains one of the most precious moments of my entire existence.

However you receive it, you will have and hold more information with that one picture than you have collected thus far, even if your adoption paperwork is reaching the four-and five-inch mark like mine had at that point. The photo is a gift. It should be cherished as one of the first tangible confirmations that this truly is happening.

Remember, sweet friend, it is happening. Even as Jesus knit your child together in his or her birth-mother's womb, He was preparing him or her for you, for your family, and for such a time as this. No matter how long you've waited, how old your child may be, or how long it will be until you are allowed to travel, know that it's all happening! Praise the Lord!

Daddy's Take:

Oh yeah! The moment we finally saw our child in a picture kind of solidified that this was really happening. After all the paperwork, praying, and waiting, it was like a gift and a promise. Take a minute to celebrate this moment with your family and support team because at this second you know you are part of a miracle, and that is amazing!

Scripture for Your Journey:

Psalm 18:19
He brought me out into a spacious place;
He rescued me because he delighted in me.

Psalm 139:13
For you created my inmost being;
you knit me together in my mother's womb.

Prayer for Your Journey:

Dear Lord,
You were there when You knit each child together in his or her birthmother's womb. This specific child, our child, was formed in Your image and is special, and we desperately desire to include this child in our family and in Your eternal family. Help us to wait for this exact child with hope and expectancy, knowing that the perfect moment to meet our new family member is coming soon. Remind us that it is a "when" and not an "if" because You are organizing every step that will bring us all together. We pray that day is soon. Amen.

Action Points:

1. If you have received your first image of your child already, share with your spouse, family, and/or accountability partner what your feelings were. Did this make the journey more real for you? Did you feel overwhelmed, grateful, or emotional in a particular way?
2. If you have not yet received your first image, I encourage you to take time to visualize that moment, however it comes. (And if your first glimpse may be in person depending on timing and situation, that's okay!)
3. I encourage you to journal about this first experience. What a wonderful gift to share with your child one day!
4. Please follow your agency or attorney's advice on sharing information or images of your child-to-be on social media. Some countries have very strict expectations, and some legal-risk situations come with their own expectations. Honor those guidelines and carry that picture with you everywhere and rejoice! You are one day closer!

NOTES

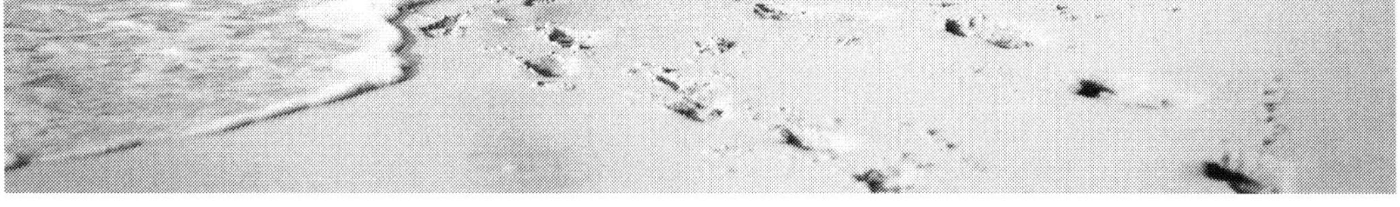

NOTES

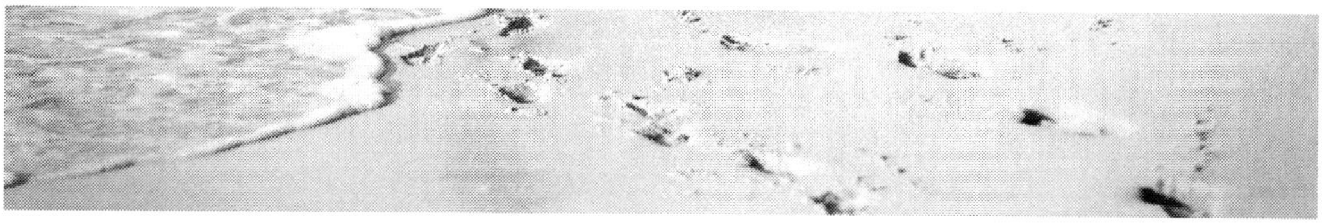

Chapter 19

WHAT TO SHARE, WHAT TO TREASURE

It is so important for you to use discretion regarding the information you share about your child's adoption, so I want to specifically hone in on that because it can involve sensitive and personal information.

I feel absolutely compelled to share this advice, not only as a mommy, but also as an adopted child myself. Pray over it, and accept it or disregard it as the Spirit leads you, but know this is coming from a heart that loves you and wants the best for you and your growing family.

Luke 2:19 states, "Mary treasured up all these things and pondered them in her heart" when the shepherds visited the newborn Jesus in Bethlehem. As a child, the Christmas story represented to me all things beautiful and special. As an adult, I now see it in a more complex light, although it is still equally beautiful. This story shows the very best God has to offer along with the hardship of the world. This story includes an unwed mother, an unexpected pregnancy, a dad having to decide whether he will leave or stay, and religious and political conflicts due to King Herod's reign. Joseph ends up becoming an everyday daddy to the King of Kings. He had a choice: He could choose to father a child or one that was not biologically his own. Our family had a choice in a similar situation with adoption. Your family has a choice, too. But when God makes the road abundantly clear to the believer, you just start walking. So first of all, kudos to every momma and daddy who were called to adoption and just started walking down the path like Joseph!

Mary's act of treasuring up these things in her heart has always stirred my mommy heart. Mary did not make it exceptionally public, which is the modern equivalent of sending out a mass email to her friends or posting it on Facebook. Scripture doesn't even say that she pestered Joseph about it to make sure she had done the right thing by her child! I mention these things because I tend toward sharing information through social media, and praise the Lord for it in many cases. Our online and personal community has aided my family multiple times by praying for coverage and protection over my children. But in the very specific realm of adoption, I want to advise caution with social media resources like Facebook, Instagram, or Twitter. These social media platforms are so public, and it is usually not appropriate to share your child's personal information this way.

If you are in pre-placement, awaiting the birth of your child, or awaiting your travel dates, then having access to loved ones far and wide is crucial. I felt that way, too. But please, please be judicious in what you share, especially with what you share in public forums. Once it is said, it cannot be unsaid. Years ago, I had an especially wise and spirit-led social worker remind me, "This is her story, not yours," in reference to my daughter's adoption story. I reared up against this, for we were, after all, discussing *my* baby! But alas, I am so grateful that I listened. There are parts of our first adoption that are precious, other-worldly, and truly show the hand of God at work, but they are also private until such a time as my oldest daughter sees fit to share them. This is hard, for I want to encourage you, and so much of her story is encouraging, but it isn't mine to share.

Because I accepted this precept early on, almost nine years later, it is fairly easy for me to recall those moments where I just saw the Holy Spirit working on her behalf; however, even knowing that it is encouraging, I want to honor and protect her. I want to respect the woman she will become and protect her from wondering about others knowing her private information. Teenagers do that often and with a variety of issues, whether adopted or biological, so why fuel the fire?

Please don't think I am being coy. I have known couples who have adopted sweet babies born from hard circumstances, such as rape. That is a really hard thing to discuss. One day, I firmly believe that a child should know his or her birth story, even the hard parts. However, the child should be able to choose whether he or she wants others to know that story. In His infinite wisdom, God reminds us "that in all things God works for the good of those who love him, who have been called according to his purpose" (Romans 8:28). Praise the Lord for that, for even the hard, messy, uncomfortable parts of our kids' stories can be used for good. We have to be patient in waiting and willing to let God use them at the time He sees fit. So please pray hard right now over how to share the hard stuff with your child one day. I want to encourage you to figure out how to share honestly, but also how to share when it is developmentally appropriate. In speaking truth, you can reclaim stolen ground from the enemy and you can guard your child's heart in the process. It's a double win!

Track with me for a moment. Imagine you are that child, now 15 or 16 years old, and are curious about where you came from, who loved and knew you first, and how adoption came to be a part of your story. Imagine finding out the hard parts at a time when you are trying to figure out what identity means, let alone who you really are. There are things in every life that can hurt, for it's part of living in a broken world. But if you go one step further, how would your heart feel if the hardest part of your beginning was something bandied about outside of your family's closest inner circle?

Would realizing that the most broken parts of your birth story and birth family were shared in detail with others bless you or break you? Would that hurt your teenage heart to realize that your adoptive parents' friends, neighbors, and acquaintances knew your story way before you did? As an adopted child myself, I can honestly admit that finding out that my parents' friends knew my business before I did would have ticked me off. It would have absolutely sent me over the edge and negatively affected the way I viewed my adoption.

Another example of details you may want to consider keeping close to heart is any difficult birth family situations, such as substance abuse that the birth mother may have chosen prenatally. These are all very personal to your child and therefore to your family. Just consider a typical toddler or teenage meltdown, and watch it through the eyes of someone who isn't intimately praying over your family but yet knows intimate details of your family. You don't want them ascribing diagnoses or labels to your kids.

On the other hand, don't hold the details so closely that things that your intimate community could rally around you for are left unsaid due to pride. If you need your people banging on the gates of heaven, then be bold, loud, and as detailed as you need to be. They are a part of this miracle and will be impacted by your family story in positive ways when they see God's faithfulness. So it is important to parent this child intentionally, prayerfully, and with an eye toward guarding his or her heart.

So really, this may be your first parenting decision for the child you are waiting to meet. You may choose to share some or none at all, and that is just fine! I know of one fine family who is waiting for their little miracle and posted a prayer request on Facebook stating, "God knows, but we need prayers for discernment and wisdom." That was fabulous. Those walking alongside that sweet couple raised them up when they needed it most, and did so knowing that the Holy Spirit would handle it in the throne room, whether they knew the details or not.

And just remember that when it comes to hard stuff we feel like we can't handle, God can handle it because He already knows. Sometimes we don't need to know. Sometimes we don't need to share.

Daddy's Take:

Because my wife is an adoptee, she takes these particular ideas to heart in a personal way. She taught me the importance of guarding our kids' stories and the importance of praying specifically about this. We have our team that even now prays us through the hard stuff, but we also closely hold specific information that each of our kids will need help processing through, for we want to honor our children, their beginnings, and this family that God has made.

Scripture for Your Journey:

Luke 2:19
Mary treasured up all these things and pondered them in her heart.

Hebrews 4:13
Nothing in all creation is hidden from God's sight. Everything is uncovered and laid bare before the eyes of him to whom we must give account.

Prayer for Your Journey:

Dear God,
Please help us steward our child's family well from the beginning. Please surround us with spiritually mature, discreet, and God-loving counsel who will speak truth over this journey. Please make us wise in what we share and how we share it. Lord, there may be some hard things that need to be

shared boldly. There may be some things we need to quietly process through. We may learn precious things that we don't know whether to share or not. Help us to discern exactly what our community needs to know and exactly what we should share just with our family. Thank You, Jesus, for our family. Thank You for writing our stories in ways that will intersect greatly with yours when we let them. Thank You for loving us. Amen.

Action Points:

1. What types of things would you consider sharing? What things would you treasure in your heart?
2. If you choose to share deeper details about harder things, whom would you share with? Make sure your spouse agrees.
3. Consider other families of whom you know too many personal details. Does your additional knowledge help or hurt the child or children involved?
4. Remember to pray hard for discernment because what is right for you and your family may not be right for another family. Your story and your child's story are being written by God. He's got this!

NOTES

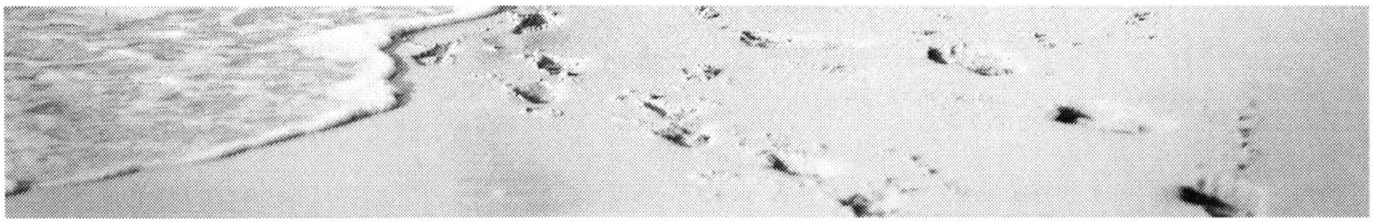

NOTES

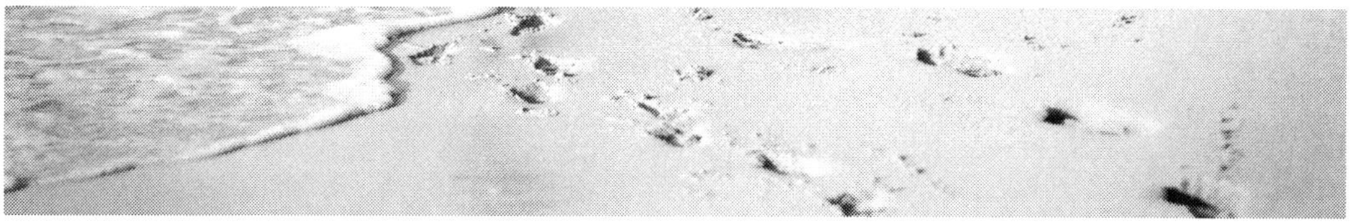

Chapter 20

PRAYING THROUGH THE LAST "TRY-MESTER"

So, you've chosen your location, submitted your paperwork, and discovered that you were matched! That is incredibly exciting. Before you read any more, take a moment or two to celebrate how far you have come.

Okay, now take a deep breath. You still have a portion of your journey left to complete!

The goal is within sight, but please, *please* do not rest on your adoption laurels. You are so very close, and I know that you have been through the wringer, likely in triplicate. But this is the time to dig deep. Because of the spiritual nature of this journey, I urge you as strongly as I can to remain prayerful and alert. First Peter 5:8 states, "Be alert and of sober mind. Your enemy the devil prowls around like a roaring lion looking for someone to devour." Be vigilant in prayer, my friend!

This last part of your journey may yet have twists and turns that you are not expecting. You are so close to the day of finalization, that glorious "gotcha day" when the government recognizes what you in your heart have always known—that this particular soul is your child, and you are his or her parent. It will happen. Continue to hold tightly to this truth: With adoption, it isn't if; it is when. But you may need to secure the breastplate of righteousness tightly around you to guard your heart, for it doesn't always feel that way. I'll share with you where we found ourselves, along with some aspects of other adoptive families' stories; however, please do not read this as a doomsday development. I pray that your journey is smooth, and that this chapter is simply a cautionary tale. I just feel that I would be remiss if I did not share with you what I found to be true in my own life and in the lives of friends whom we have been privileged to know. So just stay aware, stay hopeful, and know that if you do find yourself at the eleventh hour facing a mountain instead of an easy downhill slope, God's still got this. Here we go!

Almost four years ago, I walked into a Holiday Inn hotel room in Oklahoma and hit my knees. I sobbed my heart out, unable to catch my breath, unable to move, and I could only say over and over, "Jesus, Jesus-...please...Jesus!" My husband and my preschool-aged daughter were with me, reeling from their own heartache. There was a tangible sign of my broken dream: A seemingly innocent, white baby crib that we had ordered especially for our new baby boy was standing there. The baby boy who was supposed to occupy it was nowhere in sight. The baby boy we had been praying for years to meet, who prompted this little jaunt to the Midwest, was not present. After a three-and-a-half hour flight right in the middle of the bustling holiday season, we were unceremoniously told, "Do not come to the attorney's office. She has changed her mind and decided to parent."

The "she" in this little story is our son's birth mother, a woman we had yet to meet but had been praying for specifically for many months. The decisions she faced were daunting. I knew that the goodbye her decision would occasion would be heartbreaking. We had boarded the plane with baby clothes and diapers, thrilled that God heard our prayer and found our sweet child, but the great plan that we had all created together looked like it was about to spontaneously combust. At that moment I had to decide if I would run away from God or lean into my Savior. I leaned, broken and breaking more with each breath. But I continued to pray, only able to utter His name. I was obeying Psalm 62:8, which states, "Trust in him at all times, you people; pour out your hearts to him, for God is our refuge."

Slowly, ever so slowly, I felt the vice grip on my heart release, and I felt the Holy Spirit comforting me. Blessedly, amidst the confusion and pain that we were feeling, our daughter slept well and deeply.

The greatest surprise was when my husband's best friend and prayer partner showed up at that hotel door in the middle of America. This was surprising because he, like us, lives in the South, and he had pretty much no reason to be in that area of the country. A business trip put him within an hour or two of our hotel, and just as God provided sleep to my daughter and peace to my heart, he provided a Godly friend to speak truth and pray with my husband through that hard, hard night.

My parents also experienced difficulties toward the end of my own adoption out of Colombia in the 1970's. Actually, on the way to court to finalize my adoption in-country, my adoption paperwork flew out of the taxicab in which myself, my foster mom, and my would-be parents were riding. It didn't just flop out as a stack; it flew out in the crazy winds that Bogota is famous for, landing all across several busy streets downtown. My mother just held me on her lap and sobbed (probably much like I would sob almost 30 years later). She said the kindness of strangers astounded her. Every piece of paper was returned and they were able to reassemble it into the correct order just minutes before our case was called.

Other friends of mine have met their sweet babies only to find out that undisclosed drug use caused health issues that they had never expected. Some other friends had a paperwork glitch that misidentified their darling child as profoundly special needs, a situation that they were unprepared for and that took a certain amount of time to puzzle out.

I do not share this to scare you at all! I just want you to know that God can still be found during crunch time. In each and every case I have shared, God's will prevailed; of that I am confident.

But in every single one of the adoptions that I have been privy to be close to, God has allowed a last-minute trial, perhaps to remind the families that it really has nothing to do with them and everything to do with Him. This is a good parenting reminder, no matter how your children join your family!

So the last part of an uphill race may feel like more trial than you can bear, but you will not walk this on your own. God is with you wherever you go, and so are we, for we are praying you through this last "try-mester."

Daddy's Take:

The surprises will mount as the adoption gets closer. We can't foresee all the things that can go right or wrong—nor would we really want to. As the obstacles mounted against us, our prayer support increased in due measure. We are still in awe and overwhelmed by the many who prayed over our family and stood in the gap for us as we battled it out. We were not alone when the surprises hit, but it was still hard. I can't imagine going through all of that without the prayer team God placed around us. I wouldn't want to. I don't want to think about what could have been if our community hadn't been there for us in prayer and encouragement every step of the way.

Scripture for Your Journey:

1 Peter 5:8
Be alert and of sober mind. Your enemy the devil prowls around like a roaring lion looking for someone to devour.

Lamentations 2:19
Arise, cry out in the night,
as the watches of the night begin;
pour out your heart like water
in the presence of the Lord.
Lift up your hands to him
for the lives of your children....

Joshua 1:9
Have I not commanded you? Be strong and courageous. Do not be afraid; do not be discouraged, for the Lord your God will be with you wherever you go.

Prayer for Your Journey:

Dear Lord,
As we walk toward the end of this adoption journey, make us wise. Help us to continue our close walk with You, our close connection to our prayerful community, and our solid faith that You've got this—You really do. As the surprises mount and the wheels seem to want to fall off, let us lean into You in faith and in hope. We love You, Lord, and ask You humbly to carry us through to the breakthrough. Amen.

Action Points:

1. Talk with your spouse and your support team about how to pray through this last "try-mester." You can't foresee everything, but perhaps making a prayer tree, listing Scriptures to pray, or designating a point-person to relay needed information to will help you.

2. Think of what you will need to get through difficult discussions, delays, or setbacks. Examples could be a devotional book, your journal, or certain friends who are ready to take your calls and pray you through anything you face.
3. Talk with your spouse about how you two can stay connected through this final phase of your journey.

NOTES

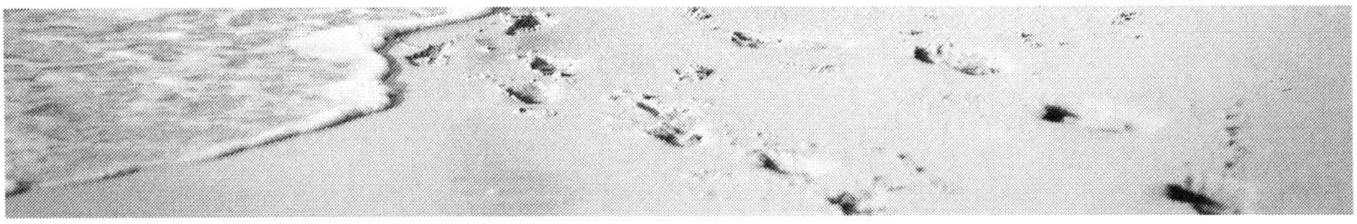

NOTES

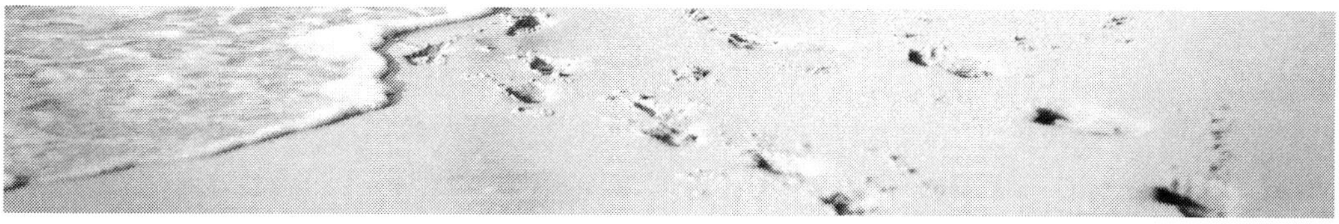

Chapter 21

POST-ADOPTION DEPRESSION

When you think of babies, children, and family, you probably feel a gentle smile spreading across your face. You may call up old memories, new dreams, or pictures of yourself at certain ages. Certainly, the way we celebrate family additions through showers, sprinkles, parties, and receptions underlines that it is not only a big deal, but it is super special.

When my parents adopted me, they held just such a reception for family and friends, just to have the joy of introducing their prayed-for child to their people. Two years later, I was a part of planning the festivities as we celebrated my younger sister's homecoming. One of the core memories of my life is what happened outside all of the organized events that day.

My baby sister, Jessica, was about nine months old. After many months in an orphanage, the onslaught of strangers, smiling and thrilled, but strangers nonetheless, probably overwhelmed her. To help her regroup, and honestly probably to show her off a bit, my daddy put her in the stroller and began to walk through our neighborhood with both of his girls. My momma, master seamstress that she was, had made matching dresses for me and Jess. Each had a soft pink underlay with a lace detailed pinafore and, to this day, it is one of my favorite outfits I've ever worn.

As we began strolling down the street, the neighborhood kids saw the fancy clothes and the proud papa's Cheshire cat grin, and gleefully joined us. In short order, we had a parade of children singing, dancing, and celebrating behind us. It was incredible.

But I have to consider the next day. After the grandparents and guests went home, my momma began the everyday mundane ministry of motherhood. I go back to the day after because I experienced my own "day after" 28 years later... and the memories of that sweet and sad time still pierce my heart.

After our family celebration with grands and guests, in-laws and outlaws, paying homage to my own prayed-for baby girl, reality set in hard. One day we were surrounded, coddled, and cared for. By that Sunday, everyone had left—as in EVERYONE.

Monday morning around 3 a.m., I woke up to a hungry baby and a hurting heart. That day I parked it on the couch and, in rapid succession, I nursed, napped, and ugly cried over and over and over. My little girl was completely dependent on me. ON ME!

Yes, we'd done paperwork, parenting classes, and interview after interview...but the actual, real-life parenting work was starting now, and I had NO IDEA what I was doing. My daughter's newborn cries pierced my soul. Was she missing her birth mom? Did she know I felt inept? Was I already failing her? Oh, my word! Where in the world did all the doubt and delirium come from!?!?

Yes, I was still praying. Yes, I was so grateful. This child was and is an answer to my heart prayer of becoming a mother. But my head and my heart were in a battle between excitement and exhaustion, between competence and total confusion.

For any momma who has ever struggled with Postpartum Depression, I am giving you a virtual hug right now. For any of you adoptive mommas who've already welcomed home your first (or second, or third) little, I pray you escaped what I've experienced more than once: Postpartum Adoption Depression.

Y'all, I am not a doctor, nor do I play one on TV, but I know what I experienced...and it was harsh and ugly. I was thrilled to be a mommy, but there was a lie whispering to me that I would fail, that her birth family would do everything better, and that I would mess this whole thing up badly.

I was too exhausted to journal, too tired to make it to a Bible study, and too low to try to reach out to my tribe. Remember, isolation is the devil's playground. Compounding all of this with the reality of my circumstances: My parents lived in another state, I lost my job because adoptions weren't given the same considerations that a biological birth was given so I was to return to work eight days after her birth, and I was just TIRED! All of this led to a very private, very sad, place of depression.

Yikes! Depression doesn't sound very happy and holy does it? And guess what, that's okay! It is okay not to be okay. Let me say that again: Even if you are deliriously joyful to welcome home your prayed-for child, it is okay for you to feel all the feels, even the yucky ones. For some of you, the exhaustion is just that, you are tired, and rightfully so. It's serious business adding a whole new person to your home. For others, you may feel a tad overwhelmed at the increase in responsibilities. Totally normal....and totally alright.

If you are like me though, your emotions may feel like a rickety roller coaster without a safety cut-off switch. You may be wildly happy and then burst into tears the next moment. There were times I would sit in my closet sobbing. I had no idea what was wrong with me, and the enemy used it to torment me.

I had these crazy thoughts that this was just my new normal, and I would not be able to reinsert myself back into real life again. I had stretches of time where I felt numb and so very alone. Looking back, I wish I had confided in someone about all the lies I was hearing and all the sadness I was experiencing. But I was so afraid to be real because the adoption wasn't final yet. I had a faulty belief that if I wasn't just glowing in public, I'd be deemed unworthy of motherhood and this dream would be ripped away.

If you or anyone you know seems to be experiencing depression for any reason, I encourage you to do three things: Pray like crazy, be there for them, and encourage them to get help. Remember, your presence is your present when a friend is struggling. Sometimes a great nap and a babysitter is the golden ticket. Some of us may need bigger guns like therapists, mommy groups, or meds. Say it with me: It's okay not to be okay. Just please know you do not have to stay there. Remember, there is Jesus, so there is ALWAYS HOPE!

God has given us an arsenal of ways to navigate the bumpier aspects of life. Be real with your spouse, your family, and your friends. You know that tribe we're always encouraging you to find? This is a fabulous moment to lean on them. Let them be your Aaron and Hur, holding you up (see Exodus 17:12–14). You do not have to fight this battle alone.

Daddy's Take:

It's probably no surprise that men and women process a lot of things differently. And that is okay. God wired us in different ways. But when I saw my wife holding the answer to our prayers, and crying heart-felt tears, I had to check myself to not fix it but also to figure out how to help her. I wasn't sure why my wife felt such sadness, but as with most things—even though I don't know what to do—the Holy Spirit knows exactly the next steps to help us. Unsurprisingly, my job wasn't to fix the situation or to fix my wife—but to be present, to "feel it" and to pray for us through it.

Scripture for Your Journey:

Exodus 17:12
When Moses' hands grew tired, they took a stone and put it under him and he sat on it. Aaron and Hur held his hands up—one on one side, one on the other—so that his hands remained steady till sunset.

Proverbs 17:17
A friend loves at all times, and a relative is born to help in adversity. ... A friend loves at all times; and a brother is born for adversity.

Prayer for Your Journey:

Jesus,
Thank you for giving to our family this gift of a child. Now we ask for help in managing the blessing. Sometimes in life we have joy and sometimes we have suffering. After so much waiting and hoping and praying, our spirits are weary.

We may experience these feelings in different ways, but when depression hits, You Lord are the answer and the antidote. When we need extra help, You have gifted us resources in counselors, in pastors, in friends, and sometimes even in medicine. Help us be wise, and let us be brave in asking for help. Thank You for always loving us. Amen.

Action Points:

1. Be real about where you are emotionally, even when it seems counterintuitive. Postpartum Depression is a real thing, and SO IS post-Adoption depression.
2. Find a mentor, a counselor, or a friend who can be accountable and encourage you. Be intentional. Set an alarm to remember to check in

with this person. Keep a journal of how you are feeling and be brave in sharing these feelings with them. Honesty helps in healing.

3. Rest—it is a Gift from God. It isn't lazy to nap, and it isn't wrong to just lie there. Embrace this gift of Sabbath and go lie supine. Pray, sleep, or just zone out. This can help re-establish a joyful mindset—and that is a good thing!

NOTES

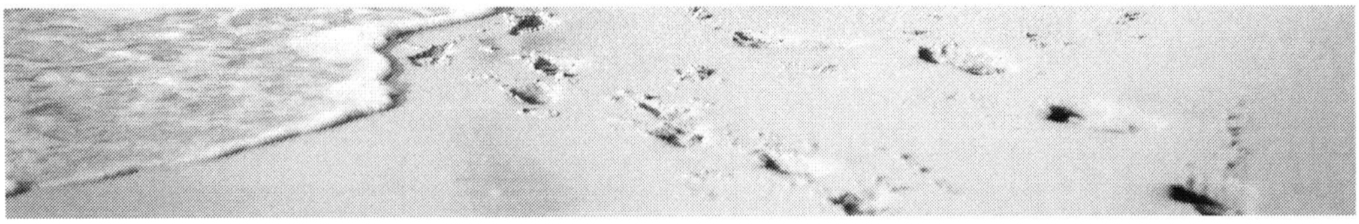

NOTES

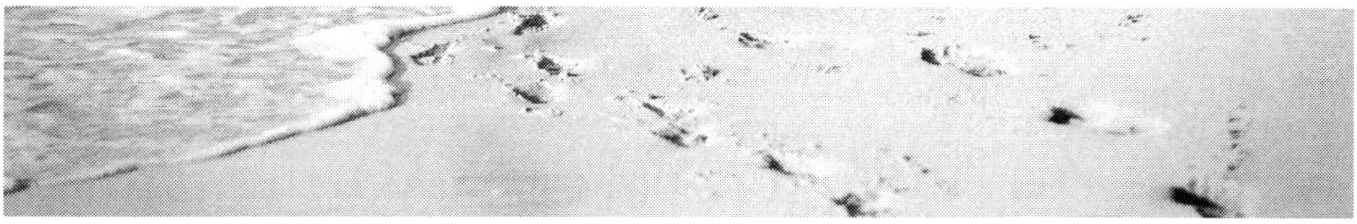

Chapter 22

SELF-CARE

Self-care is not just a nicety. It's a necessity!

A few years ago, while sitting in our marriage counselor's office, I threw a small, yet intense, conniption fit. Lest you fear our marriage is hitting dire straits, let me assure you that when you walk into orphan care, you are walking onto a battlefield, whether you know it or not. The enemy is here to steal, kill, and destroy, and we're not gonna let that happen. So, since we began this ministry, we have kept marriage counseling in the family budget. Sometimes we show up and chat about how pretty the day is and how wonderful life has been. Other times, such as the time referenced above, it is game on!

My temper tantrum erupted when the soft-spoken counselor dared to challenge me to invest time in self-care. My self-aware and not at all hostile response was, "I don't have time for self-care. I'm busy caring for everyone else." The sound of crickets filled the air. My husband and our counselor stared at me, blinking like pigeons. The absurdity of my remarks rained down upon me and, as intense as my initial negative reaction was, the truth of the words hit me hard.

"But how?" I asked these words in a frustratingly tense voice. I was running a ministry, minding a marriage, raising up our tribe of kiddos ... when and how was I supposed to find time for me? I had a list of reasons why this suggestion was ridiculous and impossible. But I also had one super important reason why I had to figure out how to accomplish this task. I was close to the breaking point and needed to regroup.

For my own spiritual and emotional health, and, honestly, for that of our family, I had to find ways to ratchet down the intensity level, find margin and white space in our super busy life, and I absolutely had to find ways not to guilt myself because of this. It is a real need, and parents are notorious for not prioritizing themselves during the marathon that is raising children. Plus, if you grew up in the church world, it sounds kind of holy to say to people that you are busy pouring into your children. But as Jesus told us in Luke 6:38, "Give, and it will be given to you. A good measure, pressed down, shaken together and running over, will be **poured into** your lap." Here's the kicker: He said it will be given to us. He didn't say He would pick it up and pour it into our minds, our hearts, our rest, and our relationships. It will be poured into our lap. And if you're anything like me, it would then pour right onto the proverbial floor as I popped up to handle another emergent non-emergency homework crisis or referee a sibling "interaction."

I was believing the lie that a good mom does all the things all the time. I forgot that God gifted us a Sabbath, a day of rest, since literally the beginning of time. If it's okay for the Almighty to take a rest, you better believe I need to do it. So, I made a deal with God. (By the way, He loves it when I bargain and negotiate!) I'd try this Sabbath thing and He'd need to redeem my time.

This was a game changer, as the four years prior to this shift I had been working 6–7 days straight. But it was a ministry, so that made it okay, right? It was necessary that I was on call should any of our families, kids, partners, churches need me in the dead of night. I began to believe the lie that I was "savior" and forgot that God invited me into this work, but can very easily do it without me.

As with parenting and all the other responsibilities that we all have before us, God has given us these gifts to steward, and He recognizes we can't do it alone. That is why He left us His word, His help (Holy Spirit), and our community to lift up our arms like Aaron and Hur (see Exodus 17:12–14) when we just can't do it anymore.

So, what does self-care look like anyway? For me it was rest, serious rest. No more working till 2 a.m. or later (earlier?). I made a bedtime and I'm sticking to it. I love to workout, so trail hikes when the weather cooperates, and Zumba or spin classes when it doesn't, have literally been a saving grace for me. As has the two hours of free child care that our gym offers its members. It also looks like weekly (yes, I said weekly) date nights with the hubs. This was another addition to our budget and it has served us well. Dates need not be fancy, and for a season most of them were home dates, eating fun or fancy foods on the back deck once the kiddos were put down for the night. (Note: I did not say asleep. It's their choice to sleep or not. It's our choice to prioritize each other.) Win-Win. They sleep when they are tired, but they know that when Mommy and Daddy have date night time, it is sacred! And they honor it!

Another thing I needed to do was prioritize my health. Unsurprisingly, late nights and balancing acts of working, motherhood and parenting, a home, and all the assorted things that come with these blessings, and I was more likely eating the remains of gluten-free macaroni and cheese or leftover pizza than I was making the foods my body needs to heal. So, as I looked at the counselor and looked into my husband's eyes, I realized—wow! I'm sick and tired of being sick and tired.

Jesus promises us an abundant life, and I was living a shadow of that promise in my efforts to do ministry and mothering 24/7.

For you, it may be friend-time, vegging out with your spouse, or taking a daily power nap. It may be bubble baths and magazines, or long walks on your own. What I learned the hard way is that when I began to make self-care a priority, I was a better momma, a better wife, and a better ministry leader than I was when I thought I was killing it. In reality. I was killing my own ability to find joy and rest and respite in the everyday mundane of life.

Am I perfect at this? No. I have to gut-check every so often to make sure my type A personality isn't getting the best of me. Sure, I was wired that way, but God has given us everything we need to be prosperous of heart and home. I just had to get, and then keep, my priorities in a God order.

I do best when I get daily time with God, weekly time with friends and family, and opportunities to unwind. Figure out what fills you up, and then schedule that in, just like a meeting or appointment. It's just as important and God already told us to rest up. So remember, caring for yourself, resting, and resetting is actually holy work, and probably one of the best things to model for the kids you love.

Daddy's Take:

Figuring out how to parent full time, in addition to everything else I need to do, such as work, taking care of our home, the cars, and the yard, I felt overwhelmed. I realized I do better at the things that matter, like being a dad, a husband, and a friend, when I take time for myself. It may be time doing woodwork, time puttering in my basement workshop, or time just listening to music or scripture by myself. The better I care for myself, the better I care for my family.

Scripture for Your Journey:

Exodus 20:8–11, NKJV
"Remember the Sabbath day, to keep it holy. Six days you shall labor and do all your work, but the seventh day is the Sabbath of the LORD your God."

Lamentations 5:22
Restore us to Yourself, O Lord, that we may be restored . . . .(ESV)

Matthew 11:28–30, NLT
"Come to Me, all who are weary and heavy-laden, and I will give you rest. Take My yoke upon you and learn from Me, for I am gentle and humble in heart, and you will find rest for your souls. For My yoke is easy and My burden is light.

Prayer for Your Journey:

Jesus,
I need Your help in remembering that it's okay to care for myself. As I care for others all day long, I know You are caring for me and I am so grateful for that. But I also know You created the idea of Sabbath and rest for a blessing. I may need help learning how to do this, but I know You can help me. Help me to find joy in the little things. Help me to refuse to feel guilty about taking care of my needs. Remind me that the healthier I am, the better I am able to care for all the things You have given me to steward. Thank You, Lord, for the gift of rest. Amen.

Action Points:

1. Find someone who loves you who will keep you accountable for your self-care. Be honest with them, check in with them, and be a partner in self-care for them as well!
2. Consider the things that give you life: time at the beach, time chatting with friends, a fire in the hearth on a chilly night. Figure out what fills you up. Make a list and have fun checking off your blessings!

3. Involve your spouse or your kids. We all need to learn how to Sabbath well. Invite them on your journey!
4. Be kind to yourself. If you are a type A personality, slowing down and resting may go against your grain. But the Sabbath isn't punishment, it is a gift and it's meant to bless each of us.

NOTES

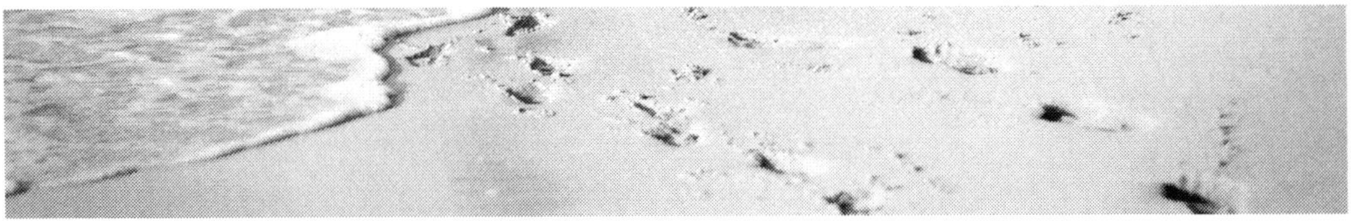

NOTES

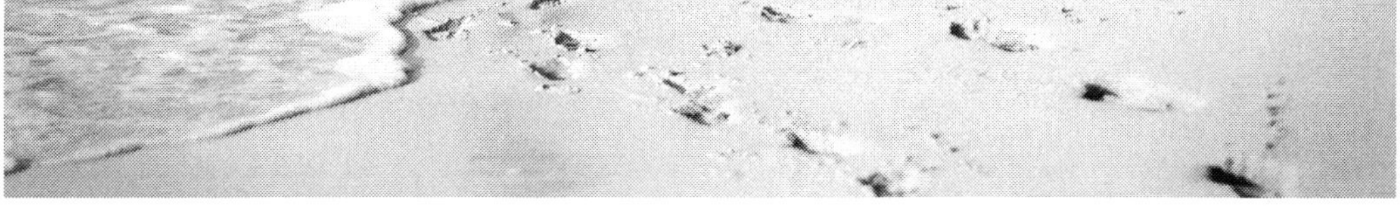

Chapter 23

ADOPTION DISRUPTION

My work as the CEO of Ignite Hope—a bridge ministry that advocates, resources, and encourages at-risk kids and those who love them—opened my eyes to the painful reality of adoption disruption. This means that the adoption fails between placement and finalization, or sometimes even after the legal aspects are complete. It broke my heart to learn that 10% of adoptions are disrupted.

Ignite Hope's calling is to rescue at-risk kids from the nightmare of life without family. One heartfelt, closely-held tenet of this ministry is that EVERY KID deserves a safe and loving home. Many of you have probably heard the term Forever Family. I have used and will continue to use this term because it is our God-goal for every child we meet.

But sometimes circumstances, trauma, and unspeakable evil overwhelm well-meaning, under-equipped families. They find themselves on a battlefield when they had expected a walk in the park. It is in moments like this that adoption disruption becomes a possibility. This is why I am a huge advocate for parent preparation and speaking authentically about the joys and difficulties surrounding the adoption or fostering process.

I share this from my heart, not to scare you or discourage you, but rather to build you up, recognizing that you are called into this by your Good Father. He sees in you a strength, a tenacity, and a heart that will meet the needs of the kid He's chosen just for you. But you cannot do this without Him.

One of my favorite sayings is, "It's not all unicorns and rainbows." I love that turn-of-phrase for a couple of reasons. First, I actually love both unicorns and rainbows. And second, because it's true! I learned this in the trenches when I battled post-adoption depression twice and then rolled right into postpartum depression a few years later. We will all hit mountains to climb in our parenting; that's a given. As Jesus promised, "In this world you will have trouble, but take heart, I have overcome the world" (John 16:33).

For some families, the typical parenting crises of colic and sleep issues ramp up to attachment and trust issues. Other adoptive parents have to navigate the mountain of drug or alcohol exposure, special needs, or other neurological surprises. But there are times when the experiences of the child and the expectation of the family just don't seem to gel. Friends, this is hard to write. I know it's hard to read. For those families who have walked through attachment, trust, and trauma issues that simply brought them to their knees, it is harder still to walk this out.

I encourage you to ask the Holy Spirit to prepare your hearts, your finances, your resources, and your people for the specific child that God has chosen for you. Be honest when you fill out the adoption paperwork, sharing those hard, unexpected details of what you can handle as a family—HIV exposure, drug addiction, human trafficking. Be real, but then be surrendered. Every one of God's kids deserves a family. EVERY ONE. Every one of God's families needs His full and precious Spirit in order to walk out their parenting journeys. Adoption ramps that need up ten-fold.

When a child has been so attacked by the enemy that labels such as unadoptable (I can't even) .... OK. I'm back. I literally had to stop and pray through that last word. That is a label from the enemy. Where the ENEMY says, "Unadoptable," GOD says, "Daughter and Son!" When the accuser of the brethren declares, "You can't do it," God reminds you that you can do all things through Christ who strengthens you (Philippians 4:13).

If you find yourself in a spot with your placement that you NEVER EVER thought you would experience, step back, hit your knees, and ask God for the resources you need. Some kiddos may need a residential placement to heal before they fully assimilate into your home. Some children may need intensive outpatient therapy. Others may thrive in a skills group or with counseling.

Be strong here as I share this nugget with you. For some kiddos, this fight is not against flesh and blood. Not at all. The scripture reminds us this in Ephesians, but for some children who have experienced or been exposed to ritualized abuse, human trafficking, and society's worst types of evil, the ministry of deliverance can be their literal saving grace...and yours as well. There is power in prayer. There is great power in praying scripture over your family. As Mom or Dad, you have every right to take authority in the heavenly realms and demand justice and freedom for your child.

My counsel here is to be wise with whomever you trust in this space to minister to the hurting heart that you parent. Make sure that they are Biblically-sound and that they are prayed up and have dealt with their own things. Pray for wisdom and discernment about who to trust with this part of your story. (Remember that the Bible promises that if we ask for wisdom, God will give us wisdom!) Ask God for breakthrough and for peace. Then...be still.

Be real with your people, health care providers, and church family. Also, lean on your social workers. They want this placement to thrive. They vetted you! They have resources you may not have considered and connections to people who can help. Be real, but be judicious in what you share and with whom you share it. Remember, this is a part of your story, but this is also your kids' story. And God is in the business of writing great stories. It will go from test to testimony one day if they choose to let it. But right now, they are living it, and so are you. Please do not share the deep details widely, as they are processing or will have to process all of this at some time in the future, and may not even be able to articulate where they are right now.

As an aside, if your family desires a strategic prayer team placed around you, please reach out to Ignite Hope, Strategic Prayer for Orphan Care. We would be honored to walk alongside you, pray over you, and encourage you as your family navigates this bumpy road (www.ignitehope.online). Walking into the messy with families in this space is why we exist. You do not have to walk this out alone.

If, after much prayer and Godly counsel, you believe God used your family as a vessel to move a child from a place of torment and abuse to a place of safety, recognize that you were obedient. Recognize that there is no condemnation for those who love Him (Romans 8:1). Hold tightly to the truth that God works all things for the good of those who love Him (Romans 8:28). Then please reach out to appropriate entities to help your child find a loving, Christ-following family who has the capacity and resources to meet that kid's needs. Making this choice does not mean you misheard God or that you have failed! Please know that this is as hard a decision as any birth mother has ever had to make. God will be with you in this hard time, just as He has been with you in the joyful ones.

Remember that institutions and bureaucracies like orphanages and foster systems are man's answers to kids without families. God's answer has always been family. God is FOR your family and for ALL of your children. Just ask Him to move the mountain and watch to see what He will do!

Daddy's Take:

There has been more than one instance in our parenting that has brought us to our knees. There have been a handful that have put us on our face...crying out to God on behalf of our kids. We were crying out for wisdom and begging God for help. No matter how you come into parenting, it will be a marathon, not a sprint. There will be great times, and there will be super hard times. But sometimes, the circumstances are far and above what a parent could expect, especially after the hard journey to get the child home through fostering or adopting.

It seems completely unfair that after all that work, issues like mental health, trauma, attachment, or a myriad of other hard things should come against you. But the enemy doesn't play fair. It's the whole reason my wife and I began Ignite Hope as a prayer ministry centered around at-risk kids and families. When you bring home kids from hard places, they have hard stuff to work through. There have been times we have been coaching families, walking alongside them, when they have had to simply surrender—to find the best place for the child they fought for and prayed for—and recognize that it may not be in their own home. That is hard stuff. It is real stuff. They may feel ostracized from their own families, from the adoption/foster community, from their church that helped support their adoption. These are the moments when I encourage them, and I'll encourage you, to lean into Jeremiah 29:11. God still has GOOD PLANS for those who love him.... Plans with hope and a future. God's good plans don't stop just because our plan was cut short. God is a God of grace for all of us. Hold on to those truths.

Scripture for your Journey:

Jeremiah 29:11
"For I know the plans I have for you," declares the LORD, "plans to prosper you and not to harm you, plans to give you a hope and a future."

Ephesians 6:12
For our struggle is not against flesh and blood, but against the rulers, against the authorities, against the powers of this dark world and against the spiritual forces of evil in the heavenly realms.

Romans 8:1
Therefore, there is now no condemnation for those who are in Christ Jesus....

Romans 8:28
And we know that in all things God works for the good of those who love him, who have been called according to his purpose.

Philippians 4:13
I can do all this through him who gives me strength.

Prayer for your Journey:

Jesus, there is so much to unpack here, and so very much that is hard to understand. We think sometimes that love will be enough to heal the brokenhearted, but the truth is ONLY YOUR LOVE and only Your grace will be sufficient. Remind us that we are not the Savior, but You are. Our job parenting any child, but especially in parenting kids from hard places, is to introduce them to the only one who can truly save them. Open our hearts to hear You. Open our eyes to see all the ways You are meeting needs, bringing resources, and aligning the next right step. Hold us gently, Father, and prepare the best places, spaces, therapies, or processes to help children heal.

We interrupt the plans of the enemy and say a holy "no" to the schemes the devil tried to put in place against vulnerable children. We thank You that You are sovereign, You are good, and You are faithful. Jesus, replace the chaos with Your peace, replace the pain with Your comfort, and redeem all the things that the enemy has stolen. In Your precious name we pray. Amen.

Action Points:

1. Make sure you are prayed up. If you are married, pray as a couple and close any open doors, so you do not give the enemy a foothold. If there is resentment, undealt with grief or anger, handle those things with Jesus in prayer and with one another in love.

2. Use your Tribe. Earlier in this guide we encouraged you to find your people—ones you trust, ones who will point you to Jesus, and ones who will walk with you in the messy and handle your hard stuff delicately. Lean into Jesus and lean on your people. Be real!
3. Look into a variety of options to meet the child's needs. Speak with pediatricians, your church's Children's Pastor, your adoption or foster care support group, or others you know and trust who have walked hard roads with children before you. Ask for their advice on who to talk with for the next steps.
4. Pray over each next step for God to bless it or block it. Trust that He will. This is not a one-size-fits-all situation, and what worked for one family or child may or may not work for you. But ask Holy Spirit to download the strategy and what you need to do. Then ask Him to bless it.
5. Self-Care. This is important and is often forgotten in times of crisis. The importance of taking care of yourself right now cannot be overstated.
6. Other-care. If you have other kids in the home, they may be suffering from something called secondary post-traumatic stress, from living in a state of crisis or severe stress. They may need counseling or prayer as well.
7. Recognize that this is a season. Ask God to deal with you gently and to make Himself known.

NOTES

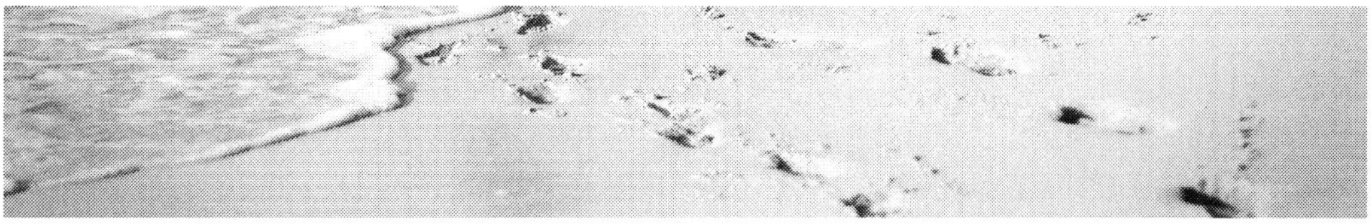

NOTES

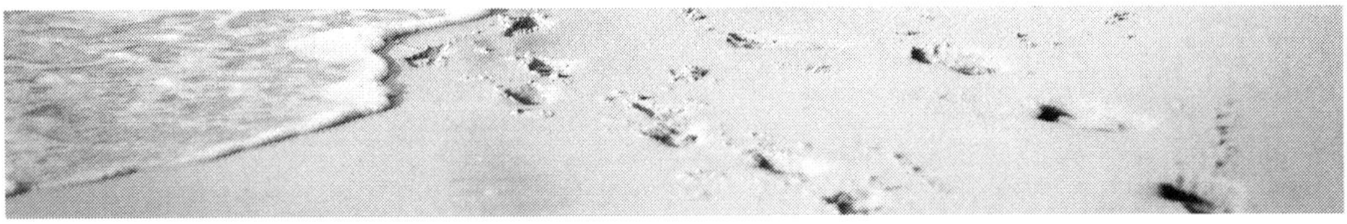

Chapter 24

ADOPTION LANGUAGE—POLITICALLY CORRECT OR "PARENTALLY" CORRECT?

First, I need to tell you that I am not always a big fan of politically correct speech, for I prefer people to speak plainly. Well, more truthfully, I enjoy when people say what they mean, and mean what they say, especially when they use some groovy adjectives or punctuation to emphasize their stance. The language-loving part of me is deeply ingrained, and this becomes helpful in adoption.

When we speak of birth parents, adoptive parents, or adopted children, I have to interject my two-cents worth of correct language; using incorrect language in such a sensitive scenario is simply not to be entertained.

As an adoptee and an adoptive momma, I can lose my mind when I hear someone casually speaking of a child being "given up." If a birth mother endured nine months of pregnancy ails and pains, felt life inside of her, and still chose to make an adoption plan, no one with any sense would say she simply "gave up" on anything! In fact, when I hear people bandying about such phrases, I never hesitate to correct them, stating, "She gave the very best she had. She gave that child all she had to give." It isn't a matter of me being right or them being wrong; it is much more personal and emotional than that. If a child hears throughout life they were "given up" at any stage, they can internalize that and project that sense of abandonment onto God.

Simple word choices can result in crucial differences in interpretation, and if you are blessed to have walked the journey of adoption and have that child in your arms, I pray so hard that your heart and mind are awakened to every possible way to guard that child's heart. Language is such a simple way to do it in a graceful and meaningful manner. No matter what anyone else says, your child will at some point look at you and remember the way you gently explained life circumstances and honored where he or she began. This is huge, and it is nothing less than any parent should do. As Proverbs 4:23 states, "Above all else, guard your heart, for everything you do flows from it." Assist your child in this!

I have had many people look at my kids and ask, "Are they your real kids?" Others have looked at my sister and asked me, "Is she your real sister?" As a daughter who was adopted, a sister with an adopted sibling, and a mom of two adopted children, to me there is nothing more insensitive or cruel than this. Adoption is a legal proceeding, and it does not define a person, relationship, or family. There are both healthy and thriving biological families and adoptive families; likewise, there are both dysfunctional biological families and adoptive families. The way children were brought into the home has very little to do with it.

Another language aspect that I must address is the word "natural." Well-meaning friends or family may sometimes identify a biological child as their "natural" child, which of course implies that the adopted child is therefore "unnatural." I counteract that by saying, "No, Christ-centered adoption is supernatural." It is better to simply educate those closest to your inner circle as to how to explain and embrace your family rather than be frustrated and offended all the time.

Included in Appendix A is an abbreviated list of positive adoption language. I urge you to pray over this, make copies as needed, and share this language with your close family and friends. Consider this to be one of your first major parenting decisions in this child's life. Yes, it may seem wordy. Yes, others might think you have jumped on the overly sensitive bandwagon. Yes, others may dismiss your efforts out of hand, but you are doing what you can to ensure a smooth transition and peaceful heart for your child. This is also a first step in welcoming your child home. You can't protect any child from everything, but at least in utilizing this type of positive language, you may protect this child from one banged up heart moment. That, like a beautiful picture, is also worth a thousand words.

Daddy's Take:

When we began this process, I realized that my wife was way more in tune with the ways words shape us than I was. When people asked if our kids were natural, I would just answer. Jacqui would boldly say, "Our kids came supernaturally—each one of them. They came with a testimony that is unique to them."

As an adoptee, my wife has reared up hard against referring to a child as being "given away." As she says, there is no giving up on a child when an adoption plan is embraced. That birth family gave everything; they gave their very best, whether they placed the child with an orphanage or an adoptive family. Now that I am also in tune with it as well, I realize the insensitivity of most of the language surrounding adoption. We pray that sharing our story helps to move the needle in people's hearts toward guarding the hearts of their children, regardless of how they came into the world.

Scripture for your Journey:

Luke 6:45
A good man brings good things out of the good stored up in his heart, and an evil man brings evil things out of the evil stored up in his heart. For the mouth speaks what the heart is full of.

Proverbs 31:8
Speak up for those who cannot speak for themselves,
for the rights of all who are destitute.

Prayer for your Journey:

Dear Lord,
We don't want to be the word police, but we do want to guard and protect the children You give us to raise. We want to let them know from the very beginning that they were not only wanted and prayed for, but that no one has ever given up on them—especially You. Make us wise with our words as we encourage others to guard children's hearts. Make us compassionate as we share as much of our story as You call us to. Guard our children's hearts always. Thank You for loving us as our Heavenly Parent. We know You understand.
Amen.

Action Points:

1. Picture your child coming to you asking why Uncle or Aunt So-and-So says his or her birth mom "gave him up." How will you respond with truth and grace?
2. Picture yourself educating Uncle and Aunt about positive adoption language before your child comes home. Isn't the extra effort or embarrassment on your part worth the guarded heart on your child's end?
3. Make a list of people in your inner circle who will be most receptive to learning this language. Compare lists with your spouse and start with these people.
4. Consider those who are close to you who do not yet understand your adoption journey and/or who may be less likely to embrace appropriate language. If these people are not ones whom you and yours could easily place boundaries around to protect your family, then pray for them to have their hearts softened and to be open to these new ideas. God is in the business of miracles, and you have your adoption journey to prove it! He can work here on your child's behalf, too!

NOTES

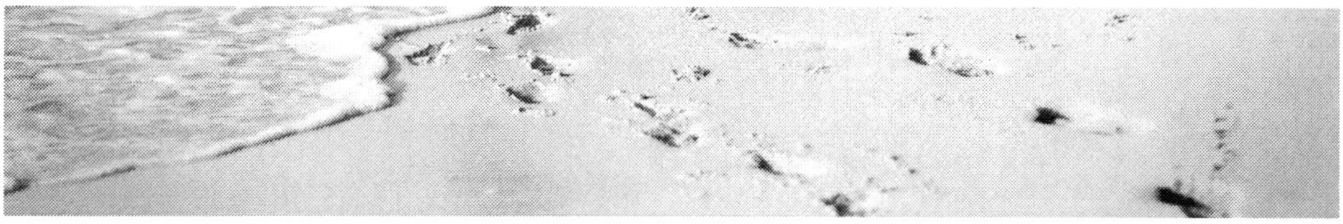

NOTES

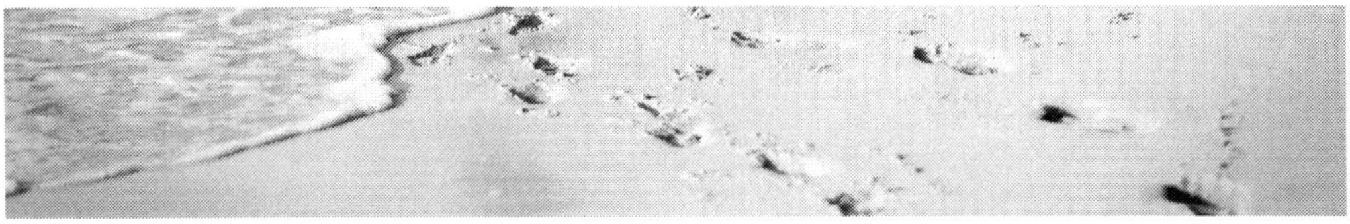

Chapter 25

SOME CLOSING THOUGHTS

At different points over the past ten years, I looked high and low to find a guidebook or devotional that would help me as I waited during the adoption of my daughter and, later, of my son. There are so many great and fabulous books on waiting, infertility, or other people's successful adoption stories. I do recommend reading these positive stories during the interim to give your weary heart encouragement! However, I was searching for something with not only spiritual meat, but also a way to practically approach our pending adoptions with hope, faith, and love. This was primarily because I became extremely beaten down with waiting.

I need my time with God or I spiral out of control. And nothing can take a waiting mommy heart on a downward spin faster than hope being delayed. Even now that my kids are home, I can still recall with glaring clarity every time my heart was challenged to cling to the hope that this was going to happen. I pray this book will provide a way for you to spend time with God and also strengthen you when you encounter obstacles.

I started to say a phrase over and over to myself, and I now share it with any family I meet who is going through an adoption process: **With adoption it isn't if; it's when!** I believe that wholeheartedly. If you are brave enough to step out in faith and obedience to start an adoption journey, and if you get those mounds of paperwork and other necessary odds and ends completed, you will have a beautiful child as the precious gift at the end of your rainbow. And for me, rainbows come to mind often when I consider all the ways adoption has touched and impacted our lives, and this is fitting because, in Scripture, the rainbow indicates God's promise He has given to you, to me, and to the orphan.

Even today, the word "orphan" is hard for me to say because it is so personal. The orphanage that represented me in my infancy actually had in its mother tongue the word "abandoned" in the title. It was accurate, descriptive, and incredibly harsh. Do not think for a moment that your child has ever been abandoned by God.

Every sweet child who was brought to an orphanage, a safe harbor spot, a baby "drop" box, or into foster care was never really abandoned, for God loved them then and loves them now. Each one of them was given life by those who knew and loved them first, they were given care by those who stood in the gap, and now they are given an opportunity when they are gifted to you!

I recognize that not every birth story, relinquishment situation, or orphanage experience is rosy, and after having worked on three continents over almost ten years on behalf of these sweet children, I am not naive enough to think that it is all unicorns and rainbows. There are hard circumstances, brokenness, and a spiritual war fought over these children's hearts. However, God is there with them through it all. He is here with you as you wonder how on earth you will afford the adoption, healthcare, education, and enrichment of this child. I know this, because He was there with me as I waited in another country, vulnerable and somewhat sick, for my parents to walk out in faith and fight the battle to bring me home.

And a few years later, He was there when my parents and I received that telegram saying that the sister I had prayed for, and the second daughter they longed for, may never come home to us.

Then thirty years later, God was by my side as I endured the longest ever drive down an unending highway, flinching with every cell phone trill, because I was certain that my dream was about to come crashing down around my ears after years of loss and waiting.

And He worked it all out, both for our good and His glory.

During this current season, our family has endured deep loss and heartache when my own Momma fought a brave battle against a rare and aggressive cancer. Walking through loss and grief is hard as an adult. Helping kids navigate their own loss and grief is heartbreaking. Recognizing that a couple of my kiddos have already experienced loss and grief, and that this new journey could trigger additional hurt, y'all, all I can do, could do, and will have to keep doing is hit my knees in prayer and raise my hands in worship. Remember, your worship is your greatest weapon. Wield it with abandon and authority on behalf of your kids. He's walking us through, and he will do it for you, too.

God didn't do that for us because we are super-spiritual or a perfect family. Truth be told, we are our own level of a hot mess much of the time.

God did it because in our hearts He whispered, "Come join me on this great adventure!" And however hesitantly or exuberantly, we obeyed. So He worked it out, just like He is doing for you now.

And you aren't doing this alone. Although I may never be able to hug your neck and personally pray with you on this side of heaven, my family and I are walking alongside you and praying you through the valleys and up the mountainside, for we know that God is working your journey out for you, too.

Mrs. Jacqui Jackson, M. Ed.
Adoptee 1976
Adoptive Sister 1980
Adopted by God 1981
Adoptive Mommy 2006, 2011
Adoption Advocate—all of my life. Amen and Amen!

Daddy's Take:

We are praying for you through every step of your journey. But more importantly, your Heavenly Father, your Good, Good Father, is walking this out with you every single step of the journey, including the exhausting and exhilarating parts. When you grow weary, lean into Him, the author of families and the finisher of your faith. You are doing good work, and children are a reward from Him. Be blessed, and know we are all cheering you on!

Scripture for your Journey:

Matthew 18:2–3
2 He called a little child to him, and placed the child among them. 3 And he said: "Truly I tell you, unless you change and become like little children, you will never enter the kingdom of heaven.

Psalm 127:3
Children are a heritage from the Lord,
offspring a reward from him.

Prayer for your Journey:

Dear Lord,
Help us remember that You are always with us. Help us remember that You are always with our child, even before we decided to adopt him or her. You love our child far more than we can begin to imagine. We pray for You to strengthen us when we are weary, to help us trust and hope in You alone, and to grow our child spiritually. We want our child to know You as the sweetest of fathers. Amen.

Action Points:

1. Journal this journey thoroughly. Save the journals to share the story of how your child joined your family. Don't just gloss over the hard stuff, although you will only want to share that at developmentally appropriate times. It's part of the story too. Sharing the hard will build trust, will grow their understanding that God gets the hard and the messy, and loves us anyways, for we all have hard and messy things in our story. Pray that God uses all the parts of this story to grow you and each of yours closer to Him. Because that's the point of all this—it's your present journey now, but soon it will be His story.
2. What do you need everyone to know about where you are in this process, how you are feeling, what you are concerned about, and the ways you have seen Jesus move?
3. What questions do others have about your adoption journey? If they aren't sure, then sharing ways they can pray and asking what they are praying for is a great starting point for this important conversation.
4. Ask your spouse and family to write letters to the birth family, orphanage, or foster family who may be caring for your sweet child. This is an incredible opportunity to share grace, the heart of the Gospel, and your heart as a parent-to-be! (I was honored to watch as one of our birth families experienced the heart of His heart right in front of me. Precious doesn't begin to cover that incredibly-timed divine privilege!)

NOTES

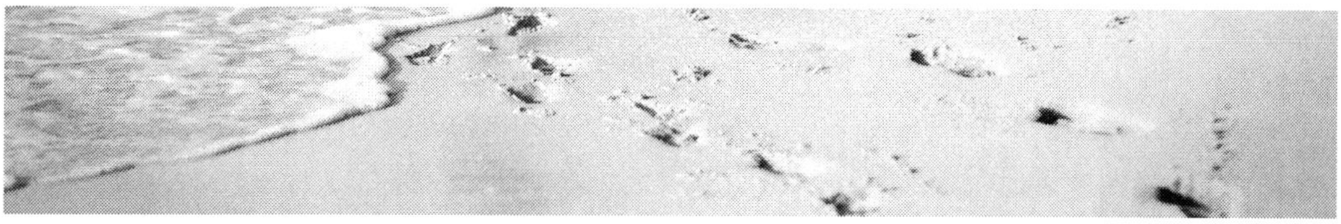

NOTES

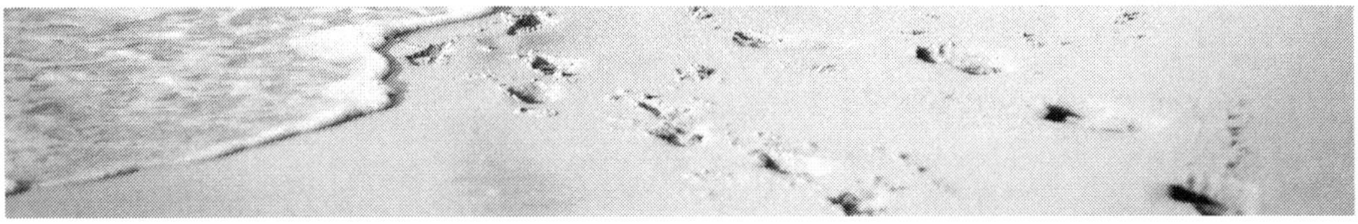

Chapter 26

ARE YOU ADOPTED TOO?

(Spoiler Alert: This may not be what you think it is!)

As I continued to pray through the second edition of this devotional, I kept feeling that something was missing. This feeling reminded me of the unsettling sensation when there is a piece of the puzzle missing. As I was working with our team and publisher, I felt the Lord nudge me gently.

Side note—I am so grateful for gentle nudges. In the past, those gentle nudges didn't always get my attention. So, what could have been a gentle leading turned into hitting a brick wall or falling off a cliff. I think God gave me a prayer ministry to run because He knows that I am a woman in desperate need of a constant, unceasing connection to my Jesus. (It certainly wasn't because I'm super holy or pray in the language of the King James Bible—because neither of those describes me!)

I've learned that the hard way, down in the trenches, where I apparently learn best. My hope is that by sharing the intimate thoughts, musings, and remembrances in this book, I can spare you some of the hard paths I've traveled, or at least let you know you're not alone as you walk your own rocky path.

So down in those trenches, flooded at times with my own tears, I learned a couple of truths. I simply cannot close out this devotional without sharing what I found there in the pit. I can tell you definitively that you will fight spiritual battles as you deal with the big hard stuff of adoption and foster care. I cannot imagine facing those challenges without the Armor of God and the friendship of His Son, Jesus Christ.

There have been times in my life where I have hit a crossroads, or more aptly, a cross in the road. God is good and grace is a gentleman. So God was not going to push His way into my life. But when I panicked, trying to decide whether to run right or left, the cross stood directly in front of me. The cross reminded me to run straight to the God who loves me, His Son who died for me, and the Spirit who wants to lead me. Through the hardest moments in my motherhood, through waiting and praying to become a momma, and now as I wait and pray to grow these little souls up into adults who love Jesus as much as He loves them, I have found that the Truth of God's love has been my literal saving grace.

We are adopted into God's kingdom. The Bible says that we are grafted into His family. At different points in my life I have both embraced and then pushed away this idea. Surprise, surprise. My willingness to accept or deny it does not discount the Truth. God calls us His children. The word "Abba" literally means "Papa"—an endearing and intimate way to say "Father." When Jesus taught His people to pray, He began with "Our Father," not "My Father."

So, if what God says is true, and what the Bible says is true, then if you have asked His Son into your life, regardless of your biological history, family of origin, or recent past, you are ADOPTED! Yes, YOU! So, as you walk out this journey, hold to that truth. God is for adoption because that was His idea. Our adoption was His big rescue plan. He loves the idea of family so much, He chose to be our Father. If you have a hard history with your own earthly father, I encourage you to find a mentor and a Bible-believing church or study and dig in. Don't let the heartache of another person keep you from walking in the fullness of your true identity as a child of God.

If the idea of a personal Jesus seems fake or far-fetched, I urge you to pick up a Bible and read the book of John in the New Testament gospels. Sometimes the world makes it seem simpler to believe in a God far away in the sky looking down on you and shaking his head, rather than the truth of a God who loves you and has numbered the hairs on your head and the days of your lives, simply because He loves you that much.

For some of us, that is an incredible blessing and maybe even a relief. For others of us, it is mind-boggling. As you read the book of John, try saying a little prayer, even silently in your heart, for God to reveal Himself to you. And, y'all, He will!

You, sweet friends, are adopted and cherished. You are wanted and loved. Nothing can say it better than this... For God SO LOVED THE WORLD (YOU!) that He gave His only begotten son, that whosoever believeth in Him shall not perish but have everlasting life. (John 3:16 KJV, emphasis mine).

So, one day when your child looks at you and asks how you can understand adoption, no matter where you started, you can honestly answer that you have been adopted. And maybe that will open a conversation with the child you've prayed home to be adopted once again, into God's family, just like they were adopted into yours...through the legacy of Love.

Daddy's Take:

My wife pretty much grew up in the church. I found Jesus later in life. No matter when or how you are introduced to the Good Father, you are invited to join His family by adoption into His Kingdom. For those of you with an earthly father who knows and loves the Lord, this may be an easier journey than for those who have experienced hurt in their families or through the church. I just encourage you to look at the scriptures listed in this book or in other Bible studies. Ask God to help you see the Truth of who He is and how much He loves you.

Scripture for Your Journey:

Luke 12:7
Indeed, the very hairs of your head are all numbered. Don't be afraid; you are worth more than many sparrows.

John 3:16, KJV
For God so loved the world, that he gave his only begotten Son, that whosoever believeth in him should not perish, but have everlasting life.

Mark 14:36
"Abba, Father," he said, "everything is possible for you. Take this cup from me. Yet not what I will, but what you will."

Action Points:

1. If you have already asked Jesus Christ to be Lord and Savior of your life, just take a moment and thank Him for this gift and for His love.

2. If you have not yet done so, consider getting baptized as an outward profession of your inward choice.
3. If you are not yet sure about the idea of your own spiritual adoption, I encourage you to take one or more of these steps.
4. Reach out to a friend who knows the Lord. Speak with them about their personal relationship with Jesus.
5. Read the book of John (fourth book in the New Testament). Ask the Holy Spirit to help you understand how this selection can speak into your life now.
6. Find a Bible believing church or Bible study near you and sit down with the pastor, priest, or lay person to talk out your concerns or questions. You can press as hard as you want on the Word of God, and it will stand up to your questions and confusion. The whole counsel of God speaks to God's love for His people—for you!
7. Ask Jesus into your Heart....

Sample Prayer:

Dear Father,
I know I sin. I mess up daily and, even though I want to do good, I can't do it on my own. But I know now that You love me no matter how messy my past or my present. I know You sent Your Son, Jesus, to die on the cross for me. I know that You love me, and I love You. I accept this huge gift and ask You to be Lord of my life, now and forever. Amen

Side note: There is no wrong way to pray. Just talk to your Heavenly Daddy and let His love surround you, in Jesus' name. Amen

NOTES

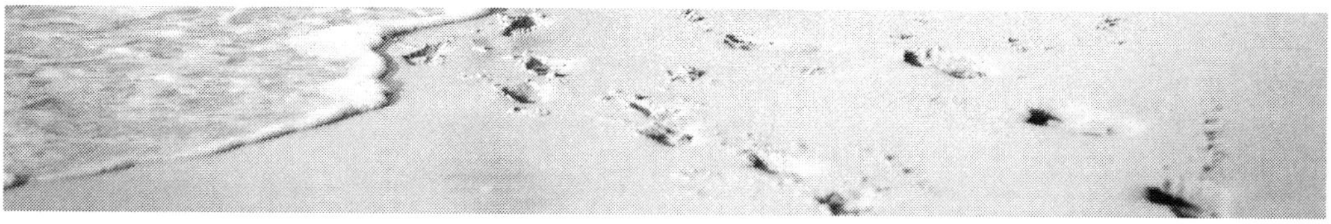

NOTES

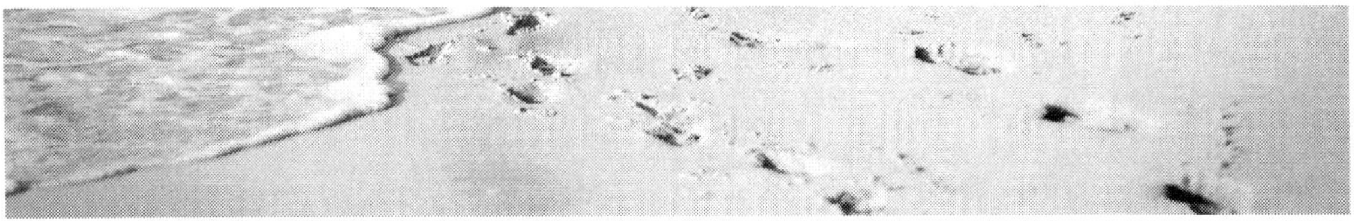

APPENDIX A

Language of Adoption

Adoption—a permanent, legally binding arrangement whereby persons other than the biological parents parent the child.[1]

Adoption agency—an organization that is licensed by a particular state to educate and prepare families to adopt children and to do all the necessary legal, administrative, and social work to ensure that adoptions are in the best interests of the children.[1]

Adoption agreement—the agreement in which the adoptive parents and birth parents put into writing their understanding of the terms of an adoption, including the degree of communication and contact they will have with each other and with the adopted child.[2]

Adoption order—the document issued by the court upon finalization of an adoption stating that the adoptee is the legal child of the adoptive parents.[1]

Adoption plan—the unique, individual plan a particular set of biological parents makes for the adoption of their child. [1]

Adoption subsidies—federal or state adoption benefits (also known as adoption assistance) designed to help offset the short and long-term costs associated with adopting children with special services.[3]

Adoption triad (aka **Adoption triangle**)—an expression used to describe the three-sided inter-relationships among adopted children, their birth parents, and their adoptive parents.[2]

Adoptive parents—a person or persons who become the permanent parents with all the social and legal rights and responsibilities incumbent upon any parent.[1]

At-risk placement—the placement of a child into the prospective adoptive family before the rights of the birth parents have been legally extinguished.[2]

Biological family—the parents and siblings who are genetically related to a child.[4]

Biblical orphan—refers to orphans in biblical times who were often left parentless because of disease or war.[4]

Birth certificate—a certified document that indicates the birth information of a person including the mother's and father's names and the name given to the child at the time of birth. Once the adoption is finalized, the original birth certificate is amended to reflect the adoptive parents as the child's parents and the original birth certificate is sealed.[1]

Birth parent—a mother or father who is genetically related to the child.[1]

Certified copy—a copy of an official document, like a birth certificate, marriage certificate, or divorce decree, that has been certified by an official to be authentic and bears an original seal or embossed design.[1]

Confidential adoption (aka **Closed adoption**)—an adoption in which the birth parents and the adoptive parents do not meet, do not exchange identifying information, and do not maintain contact with each other.[1]

Cooperative adoption (aka **Open adoption**)—an adoption in which the birth parents and adoptive parents have contact with each other before and/or after the placement of the adopted child.[1]

Designated adoption (aka **Identified adoption**)—an adoption in which the birth parents choose the adoptive parents for the child.[1]

Domestic adoption—an adoption that involves the adoptive parents and a child that are permanent residents of the United States.[1]

Dossier—a collection of required documents that is sent to a foreign country in order to process the adoption of a child in that country's legal system.[1]

Employer Adoption Benefit Package—adoption benefits provided to employees as part of an employer-sponsored benefit program, which are included within their employment compensation package.[1]

Facilitator—an individual that is not licensed in an adoption agency or as an attorney, and who is engaged in matching biological parents with adoptive parents.[1]

Finalization—the legal process by which the adoption becomes permanent and binding.[1]

Forever family—the family a child is placed with permanently, usually used in terms of adoption.[4]

Hague Convention—a multinational agreement designed to promote the uniformity and efficiency of international adoptions.[1]

Home study (aka **Family profile**)—an in-depth review that the prospective adoptive parents must complete to be able to legally adopt. A home study typically includes inspections of the adoptive parents' residence; evaluations of their relationships, parenting ideals, medical history, employment verification, and financial status; and criminal background checks. Home studies can become outdated, and typically needed to be renewed after one year.[1]

Home visit—an inspection of the adoptive parents' residence.[1]

Independent adoption—an adoption arranged privately between the birth family and the adoptive family without an adoption agency.[1]

International adoption (aka **Inter-country adoption**)—the adoption of a child from a country outside the United States.[1]

Interstate Compact for the Placement of Children (ICPC)—If a child is born in a state other than where the prospective adoptive parents reside, the Interstate Compact of both the baby's home state and the prospective adoptive parents' home state must give their approval before the child travels (for the purpose of adoption) to the state where the prospective adoptive parents reside. The agency with custody of the child is responsible for processing the interstate paperwork.[1]

Legally free for adoption—refers to a child's status when the parental rights of both birth parents have been terminated by the court and all appeals have been exhausted.[3]

Life book—a pictorial and written representation of the child's life designed to help the child understand his or her unique background and history. The life book usually includes input by or information on birth parents, other relatives, birthplaces, and birthdate, and can be put together by social workers or foster or adoptive parents working with the child.[3]

Match (aka **Matching**)—the process of bringing together qualified prospective adoptive parents and willing biological parents, who choose to explore the compatibility of each other and who can agree on the terms under which the adoptive parents can adopt the child.[1]

Modern orphan—refers to today's at-risk children who usually face high levels of addiction, substance abuse, negligence, and abandonment in their biological families; contrasts with the connotation of "orphan" in relation to war and disease alone.[4]

Placement—a term used to describe the point in time when the child comes to live with the adoptive parents in their home.[4]

Post-placement services—a variety of services provided after the adoption is finalized, including counseling, social services, and adoptive family events and outings.[1]

Revocation of consent—when a biological parent revokes the consent they had signed to an adoption and requests that the child be returned to his/her custody.[1]

Semi-open adoption—occurs when the potential biological mother or biological families experience non-identifying interaction with the adoptive family. In most cases, the interaction is facilitated by a third party who is usually an adoption agency or adoption attorney.[1]

Surrender—the legal documents signed by the biological parents in which they place their child with an adoption agency who in turn places the child with the adoptive family that the biological family chooses. In some states this may be referred to as "relinquishment" or "consent."[1]

Tax Credit (adoption)—a tax credit for qualifying expenses paid to adopt an eligible child. The adoption credit is an amount subtracted from the adoptive parents' tax liability.[1]

Termination of parental rights—the process by which parent's rights to his or her child are legally and permanently terminated, after which the child becomes eligible for adoption.[1]

U.S Citizenship and Immigration Services Bureau (**USCIS**)—an agency of the federal government that approves an adopted child's immigration into the United States and grants the U.S. citizenship to children adopted from other countries.[1]

Waiting child—a child currently available for adoption. Waiting children may be in the U.S foster care system. They might be older and could be children with special needs.[2]

Vulnerable children—groups of children that experience negative outcomes, such as the loss of their education, morbidity, and malnutrition, at higher rates than do their peers.[5]

[1] http://www.friendsinadoption.org/adoption-resources/for-potential-adoptive-parents/resources-for-adoptive-families/adoption-terms/.
[2] http://family.findlaw.com/adoption/glossary-of-adoption-terms.html.
[3] https://davethomasfoundation.org/adoption-guide/terms.
[4] https://www.ignitehope.online/
[5] http://info.worldbank.org/etools/docs/library/164047/howknow/definitions.htm.

LIST OF BIBLE VERSES BY CHAPTER

Chapter/Bible Verses

1 Psalm 139:14, Proverbs 3:5–6, Isaiah 61:3, Joshua 1:9
2 James 1:27, Hebrews 12:1–2, Exodus 2:10, Deuteronomy 1:30
3 James 1:5–6, Psalm 25:4–5, Psalm 31:3
4 Proverbs 3:5–6, Joshua 3:15–16, Psalm 32:8
5 Philippines 4:13, Psalm 68:6
6 Jeremiah 1:5, Psalm 100:3
7 Job 29:11–12, Ecclesiastes 4:12, Zephaniah 3:17
8 Romans 12:12, Philippians 4:6–7
9 Psalm 34:18, John 10:10, Lamentations 3:22–23, John 16:33, Exodus 14:14
10 I Thessalonians 5:8, 2 Chronicles 20:17
11 Psalm 46:10, Ecclesiastes 3:1, 2 Corinthians 10:5
12 Psalm 27:14, Galatians 6:9
13 Exodus 17:11–12, Psalm 46:10, Esther 4:14
14 Proverbs 3:6, Jeremiah 29:11
15 Mark 4:39, Isaiah 55:8, Psalm 100:5, Matthew 18:6, James 1:27
16 Luke 14:25–26, Job 12:13
17 Proverbs 4:23, Romans 8:28–29
18 Psalm 18:19, Psalm 139:13
19 Luke 2:19, Hebrews 4:13
20 1 Peter 5:8, Psalm 62:8, Lamentations 2:19, Joshua 1:9
21 Exodus 17:12–14, Proverbs 17:17
22 Luke 6:38, Exodus 17:12–14, Exodus 20:8–11, Lamentations 5:22, Matthew 11:28–30
23 Jeremiah 29:11, John 16:33, Romans 8:1, Romans 8:28, Philippians 4:13
24 Proverbs 4:23, Luke 6:45, Proverbs 31:8
25 Matthew 18:2–3, Psalm 127:3
26 John 3:16, Luke 12:7, Mark 14:36

ACKNOWLEDGEMENTS

I want to take a moment to thank the people who made this book possible. First, all my love and big squeezes to my incredible prayer partner, best friend, and husband—Jeff Jackson. There is no way I could do this great, big, crazy, beautiful life without you right next to me. I love you dearly for always.

Thank you to our children who gave me the gift of motherhood and continue to bring me greater joy than any of you will ever know. We love y'all to the moon and back—and Jesus loves you even more than that.

Thank you to my parents for stepping out in faith to walk out my adoption process, and then again to go find my soulmate and sister—J. Thank you for introducing us to Jesus and for beginning that legacy of faith throughout our family. I couldn't love y'all more.

Thank you to the entire Ignite Hope team for challenging me to grow outside my comfort zone, and to learn how to listen to Holy Spirit with my whole heart. Your love for God and at-risk kids makes our work possible, and I am grateful every day that I can call each of you teammates and friends.

Thank you so very much to Rhonda Fleming, my publisher, who encouraged me to move forward with this project, which ended up being much bigger and much more involved than either of us thought at the beginning.

All my thanks to Alyson Rockhold, editor and encourager extraordinaire. You take my rabbit trail thoughts and help craft them into something way more than I could do on my own. You are a treasure and I am grateful to God for bringing you into the Ignite Hope family and into our lives.

Most importantly, I thank my Lord and Savior Jesus Christ for Your gift of eternal life, daughtership, and an understanding of what a Good Father truly is. I pray that somehow this small offering impacts families and kids for You, and that You will take this and multiply it in whatever way You desire. I love You.

ABOUT THE AUTHOR

Jacqui Jackson, co-founder and CEO of Atlanta-based nonprofit Ignite Hope, is a former foster kid, an international adoptee from South America, and a grateful mommy to a tribe of heart babies and belly babies alike. Her relentless passion for adoption and fostering arises from the legacy God has given her to steward for His glory: encouraging and equipping others to walk their own journeys caring for at-risk kids.

Her initial steps towards protecting vulnerable children began in college when she chose championing at-risk kids as her platform issue while competing in the Miss America Organization. Jacqui used the scholarships earned during those years to attain undergraduate degrees in Journalism, Mass Communication, and Elementary Education. She achieved Summa Cum Laude status in her Master's of Education program where she focused on education in urban/at-risk environments.

Jacqui has professional experience as the public relations liaison for the Atlanta Hispanic Chamber of Commerce, a grant writer for the Georgia Family Council, and as an educator who worked with students ranging from pre-k to college level in Title I public schools, private schools, and in homeschool co-op environments. All of her academic and professional experiences solidified her dedication to be the voice of at-risk children in the public square and straight to the heart of God.

After becoming a first-time mother through the gift of adoption, Jacqui knew she had found her heart's desire: to be a mother to many and a child welfare advocate. When she isn't writing, speaking, or promoting Ignite Hope, Jacqui is passionate about shaping legislation that will impact at-risk kids, human trafficking issues, kids in foster care, and families in crisis.

Jacqui leverages her personal story as an adoptee and adoptive mother to encourage and empower families caring for at-risk kids, and to speak into the lives of at-risk children, because Ignite Hope was founded to reclaim stolen ground from the enemy in the space of orphan care. To that end, Jacqui believes that every one of us has been called to ignite hope.

Jacqui and her husband Jeff live in the suburbs of Atlanta along with their tribe of heart babies, belly babies, and one fur baby named Jelly Bean—a therapy dog in the making. The entire family is active in their local church and community, from serving and soccer, to dance classes and family fun nights. When she is not chauffeuring kids to activities or managing their virtual schooling, Jacqui enjoys reading (Francine Rivers!), Zumba, and trail hiking.

Connect with Jacqui:
Website/Blog: http://www.ignitehope.online/
Facebook: https://www.facebook.com/ihope4orphans/
Twitter: https://twitter.com/ihope4orphans
Linkedin: https://www.linkedin.com/in/jacqui-jackson-ignite-hope/

IGNITEHOPE
STRATEGIC PRAYER FOR ORPHAN CARE

Ignite Hope exists to rescue at-risk kids from the nightmare of life without family. We work pre-born to permanency in the public square and straight to the heart of God to strategically impact the lives of children at risk.

Ignite Hope advocates, resources, and encourages in the space of child welfare—working as a bridge to advocate legislatively and within the church to ensure that every at-risk child and those who care for them are resourced and informed of best practices.

Join our work!

You can reclaim ground stolen from the enemy and win the war targeting at-risk kids!

How?

Join the Ignite Hope team by:

- Connecting Ignite Hope with your local church, school or organization
- Connecting Ignite Hope with colleges for internships through our Campus Ambassador Program
- Joining one of our Ignite Hope prayer teams—covering child welfare needs personally, politically, and regionally
- Enabling content development, family coaching, and training through your one-time or monthly financial gift by giving at www.ignitehope.online/donate

Every kid is one caring adult away from becoming a success story. You can be the spark that Ignites Hope!

Before You Say Good-bye...
When you close this book, we hope you will take the opportunity to review it on the website where you purchased it, or share your thoughts on social media. If you believe the book has value and is worth sharing, would you take a few seconds to let your friends know about it? If it turns out they like it, they'll be grateful to you, and so will I.

Made in the USA
Columbia, SC
04 May 2022

59946264R00117